The Long Walk Home

Buen Camino!
Marcia Wakeland

The Long Walk Home

Confessions on the Camino

Marcia A. Wakeland

EMBER PRESS

PALMER, ALASKA

Cover and book design by NANETTE STEVENSON
Copy editing by JOETH ZUCCO
Proofreading by MELISSA ALGER
Photo prepress by STEVE ORF
Cartography by MAPPING SOLUTIONS, ANCHORAGE, ALASKA

Printed in the U.S.A.
www.emberpressbooks.com

Front cover photo courtesy of Randall Durrum
Back cover photo courtesy of Photo 11199532 © Lianem | Dreamstime.com
Frontis photo courtesy of Photo 45580435 © Roberto Atencia Gutierrez | Dreamstime.com

Library of Congress Cataloging-in-Publication Data
Names: Wakeland, Marcia A., author.
Title: The long walk home: confessions on the Camino / Marcia A. Wakeland.
Description: Palmer, Alaska: Ember Press, 2022. | Summary: "As a pastor who had recently left parish ministry, Marcia A. Wakeland wondered how she had once felt so profoundly called to that ministry but now found herself with big questions about her faith. She and her husband set out on the famous Camino de Santiago, the Way of St. James, on a pilgrimage to help sort through the contradictions of her spiritual journey. *The Long Walk Home* is a testament to one woman's courage to confront herself, her faith, and to finally stand unexpectedly on Holy Ground"—Provided by publisher.

Identifiers: LCCN 2022009943 (print) | LCCN 2022009944 (ebook)
ISBN 9780998688374 (trade paperback) | ISBN 9780998688381 (ebook)

Subjects: LCSH: Wakeland, Marcia A.—Travel—Camino de Santiago de Compostela. | Christian pilgrims and pilgrimages—Spain—Santiago de Compostela. | Christian biography—United States. | Camino de Santiago de Compostela—Description and travel.
Classification: LCC BV5067 .W345 2022 (print) | LCC BV5067 (ebook)
DDC 263/.0424611—dc23/eng/20220330
LC record available at https://lccn.loc.gov/2022009943

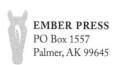

EMBER PRESS
PO Box 1557
Palmer, AK 99645

To Steve,
who has walked beside me these many years,
with a heart for adventure and a love of wilderness.

And to my mother, Marilyn,
who taught me to love words and walk in faith.

Contents

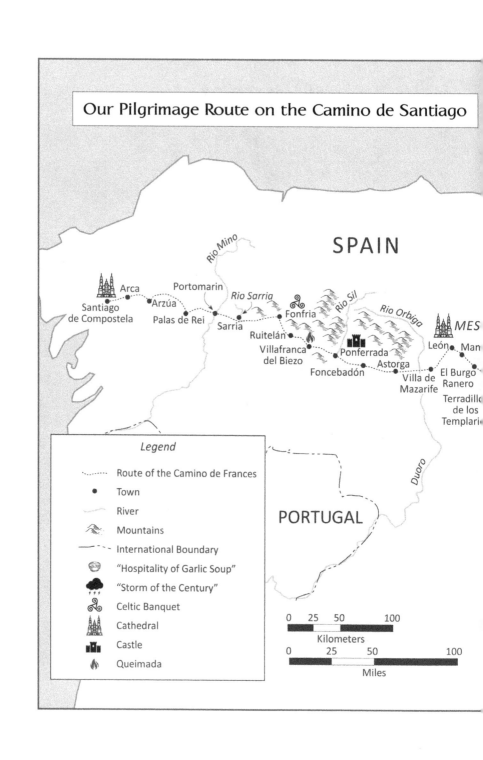

Our Pilgrimage Route on the Camino de Santiago

SPAIN

Rio Mino

Arca
Portomarin
Rio Sarria
Santiago
de Compostela
Arzúa
Palas de Rei
Sarria
Fonfria
Rio Sil
Rio Orbiga
MES
Ruitelán
León
Man
Villafranca
del Biezo
Ponferrada
Astorga
Foncebadón
Villa de
Mazarife
El Burgo
Ranero
Terradill
de los
Templari

PORTUGAL

Duoro

Legend

.... Route of the Camino de Frances

• Town

— River

🗻 Mountains

- - - International Boundary

🍲 "Hospitality of Garlic Soup"

⛈ "Storm of the Century"

🌀 Celtic Banquet

🏛 Cathedral

🏰 Castle

🔥 Queimada

| 0 | 25 | 50 | 100 |
Kilometers

| 0 | 25 | 50 | 100 |
Miles

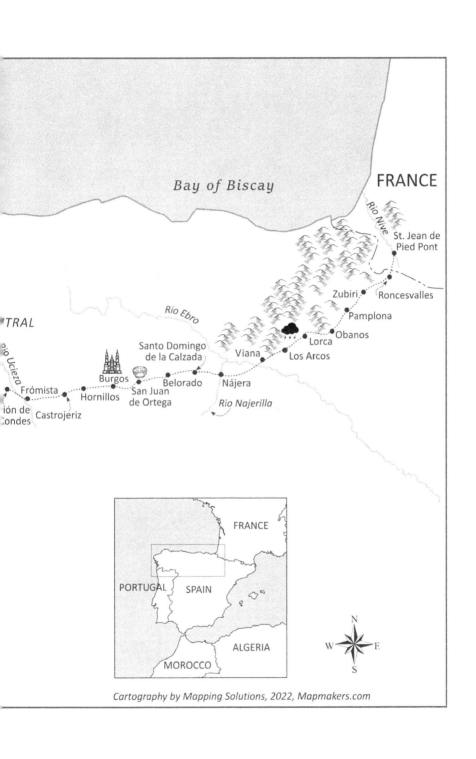

Bay of Biscay

FRANCE

Rio Nive

St. Jean de
Pied Pont

Roncesvalles

Zubiri

Pamplona

Rio Ebro

Obanos

TRAL

Lorca

Santo Domingo
de la Calzada

Viana

Los Arcos

Rio Ucieza

Frómista

Burgos

Belorado

Nájera

Hornillos

San Juan
de Ortega

ión de
Condes

Castrojeriz

Rio Najerilla

FRANCE

PORTUGAL

SPAIN

ALGERIA

MOROCCO

N
W   E
S

Cartography by Mapping Solutions, 2022, Mapmakers.com

The Long Walk Home

My soul yearns for your presence;
my whole body longs for your light.

Psalm 84

Chapter 1

The Invitation

We had slept on a cold stone floor the night before with our wet clothes on in our sleeping bags, hoping they would dry. We ached for a hot cup of coffee or tea in the morning, but it was a holiday and all the cafés were still closed at seven o'clock. Another rainy day, but now the wind was blowing us sideways as we walked the muddy path. Even then we refused to take the shortcut and walk on the highway to the next town as other pilgrims were choosing to do. No, we would take the more difficult way and stay on the trail. At that point in our monthlong pilgrimage on the Camino de Santiago, we still had our pride.

An hour or two into the trek that day, the path dipped down into a steep ravine, the water gushed over the trail, turning it to a red, thick clay. Midway down I slipped, falling forward and landing face-first in the mud. On impact, my pack was thrown over my head, pinning my face into small sharp rocks and mud. And just for a moment I laid still, feeling the water trickling by my face, thinking, *Remember, this was your dream.*

The dream had begun over a year earlier on a weekend retreat in Anchorage led by a Catholic nun named Joyce Rupp. It was February 2006. On the first night of that retreat I learned that Joyce had walked the Camino de Santiago, a pilgrimage route dating back to the Middle Ages and had written a book about it—*Walk in a Relaxed Manner.* The retreat itself didn't center on her pilgrimage, but some of the participants had come on the first night just to hear her speak about the Camino and had their own stories to share with me.

"We've walked it twice and will walk again," said a woman with a French accent and wispy, exotic hair. "You must do it, *cherie*. It will change your life. Call us, and we will tell you everything." With that intriguing invitation, and the way Joyce Rupp spoke of her walk, I came alive thinking about walking a pilgrimage. Would this bring me the clarity I was hoping for right then in my life? Joyce had described her own walk as one where the simple act of walking in a sacred manner had opened her heart and cleared her mind.

But could I even physically do it? The stress and demands of my current work had left me with frequent migraines, and my old back injury was so much worse that I was limping around the office. My body was telling me to listen. Something had to change.

That night at the retreat center I had a dream about walking down a long hallway, looking for a shower. In my journal I wrote:

> I am opening doors of rooms where I don't belong. In the last room I throw heavy things that I was carrying on my back. I am aware that there is a fire behind me, burning things up, but I am not concerned. Then I came to a turn in the hallway, and the floor is white tile with scooped out places in them that look like scallop shells. In my dream, I said, "This is hard walking, but it is so beautiful." After that turn, I find the shower, the water.

I bought Joyce's book and took it home to read after the retreat ended. Within a few pages, I was startled. She wrote that the way of the Camino is marked by scallop shells! I sat up in bed and thought of my dream. I hadn't known this at the time, and yet I had dreamt of a road of scallop shells where I was throwing away heavy things I was carrying and a fire burned them up behind me. Was this a metaphor for a turning point in my life? Immediately the thought came and stayed, *I am supposed to walk this pilgrimage. I don't know why, I don't know how, or when, but I am.* It seemed quite an undertaking to do alone, especially with my unstable back. The route she had taken was the most popular of the many paths to Santiago—the Camino Frances. It was a five-hundred-mile journey over mountains, then a flat mesa, and then over mountains again.

My husband, Steve, would be the perfect companion—one who never complains in the worst of times and laughs a lot the rest of the time. We met at an avalanche rescue training seminar looking for fake bodies in snow. Our relationship had been an adventure from the start. When I told him about the Camino and my dream, he didn't scoff or think I was crazy. He was immediately interested. We had been hiking together all over the mountains in Alaska for twenty-seven years and knew we traveled well together. He had never been to Europe and that interested him too. We began to seriously consider going on pilgrimage.

A few days after I asked him about walking the Camino, he happened to mention it at the local lumberyard where he goes for coffee every morning. Much to his surprise, one of the gruff clerks who has a reputation for a foul mouth, said, "The Camino? I've walked it. You should do it. It'll change your life." Steve was so amazed that this fellow knew about it and had been so impacted by the journey that Steve became more enthusiastic. But he had houses to build, and it would be several months before his contracts were met. And I had a big congregation to serve. We couldn't go on a six-week trip right now.

Yet it was hard for me to think about waiting. I was so restless and unsettled about my work as a parish pastor. It had been five years since I took my first call; I had sacrificed so much to achieve this second career, thrown myself into the work of it, and now I was often thinking of leaving. I needed some time away to see if it was just compassion fatigue or was the call itself no longer sincere? That thought roused so much sadness.

But underneath that question was a deeper one prowling around, like a tiger lurking in the shadows, just wanting to be asked; *maybe this restlessness wasn't so much about this particular call or this particular role.*

Maybe it was that agitation that St. Augustine spoke of when he wrote, "We are restless until we find our rest in Thee." I knew that even though I preached about trusting God, surrendering to God, loving God, I wasn't really experiencing God. My call had become fervent words of faith, but my role as a pastor had not made me feel closer to the Beloved. Why? What was keeping me from that which I most desired?

It was those very barriers that the Camino would literally shove into my face along the journey to come.

"Travelers go out in the world with their devices and prejudices intact to smooth their journeys," writes Laura Prior-Palmer who had her own pilgrimage of sorts on horseback in Mongolia. Yet, in her book, *Rough Magic,* she points out, "Etymologically a traveler is one who suffers (travail). The traveler forgets she's going home, and forgets herself too."

I knew that there would be physical suffering on the Camino. I was ready for that travail of fatigue and sore feet. But I was more reluctant to experience the travail that would be revealed about the shadow side of me, the parts I didn't want to own. That was the part about transformation on pilgrimage—leaving the familiar ways, discarding my "devices and prejudices," and as everyone seemed to report, "changing my life." Perhaps I had forgotten parts of myself in the role of pastor, where I needed to be a lot of things for a lot of people. Had I forgotten myself as a traveler on this earth as Prior-Palmer suggested?

And what did she mean that a "traveler forgets she's going home?" It didn't seem like something I could forget. For in taking this step to go on pilgrimage, I sensed I was looking for just that very thing—finding a home within myself that was at ease and content.

If a traveler "forgets herself," the self I wanted to forget was contained in the heavy things I was carrying on my back and throwing into rooms in the dream I had on that retreat. I wanted to throw away the parts of self that no longer served, subdue my ego, and then see what was left. What self would explore and walk around the next corner? Who was that I?

Just a month after that retreat, a different and unexpected invitation came for me to travel to Europe with a friend. I wouldn't have to wait until next year to take a brief sabbatical from my work. I would have that respite sooner than later after all. It would be a pilgrimage—although I didn't recognize it at the time. It was the preparation I would need for the Camino—and my long walk home.

*There is a wide door . . . opening to me
and there are many adversaries.*

1 Corinthians 16:9

Chapter 2

Hidden Doors

My friend Nanette was going on her annual trip to Verona to supervise the printing of her client's nature calendars. She welcomed a companion but warned me she would be gone most of the time. I assured her this was perfect. I needed the time alone to just wander and settle and find some rest and clarity with all these questions about my role as pastor and, deeper yet, the discontent of my soul. What was this feeling of disenchantment with the church that was so much a part of my tradition, my culture, my memories, and my consolation? Why did the fire of my calling feel like a candle in the wind now? Yet I could also acknowledge that there was a history of questioning the church and its theology.

I loved going to church, even as a child. I did my share of squirming in the hard wooden pew and hoping the sermon would be shorter. But I wanted to go. It was where I felt I belonged. I knew who I was and what was expected. I was part of a close-knit farming community at St. Paul Lutheran Church that relied on their faith and the good earth to make it through the days of their lives. I loved learning about God, singing in the choir, and going to Sunday School. I went eagerly to the church cemetery to visit the graves of my ancestors. My great-great-grandfather's name was inscribed there on the charter of the church and my great-great-grandmother's hands helped clean and bake for this church back when every other Sunday's sermon was still in German. I was the one to make a little altar in the closet of my room when I was a child. Even as a teenager I would be the one to find a church if I was on vacation with friends. I never missed a Sunday or a special service during my years at home. My soul would lift as the candles were being lit, as Mrs. Folkerts swayed as she played the organ to a crescendo, or the way my father's big calloused finger would trace the verses of the hymn so I could follow. I would be the one to sneak into the chapel for a few minutes at college when I felt unsure or alone.

My first real dissonance with the church began when I dared to ask a question in confirmation class—the two-year program for seventh and eighth graders before they could "confirm" they wanted to be members of the church and then be able to take Holy Communion.

The pastor was teaching us how to avoid breaking the second commandment: "Do not take the name of the Lord your God in vain." He was delineating what he felt constituted swearing. Of course, we knew better than to ever let the word *damn* cross our lips, let alone *God dammit*, as we would be sending someone straight to hell. But when he asserted that we should not say *Jiminy Cricket* when we were angry, I was puzzled.

"Don't you see?" he said, "that's the initials of Jesus Christ, and just another way of using his name in vain."

I raised my hand cautiously. Something didn't make sense to me. "But I am not intending to take Jesus's name in vain," said my thirteen-year-old self. "I don't think, *Jesus Christ* when I say it. I think of *Jiminy Cricket*. So is it really wrong if that is not my intention?"

I watched as his face turned red, and I could see he was struggling to control himself. I'm still not sure to this day if it was because I questioned his authority or if he had such strong convictions. Maybe both. At any rate, my question was not received well; it was disregarded. He went on to specify that we should not say Jiminy Cricket, and we couldn't say *gee* or *geez* either because that was a shortened form of Jesus, and we also couldn't say *criminy sakes*, which was a version of saying Christ. I was a bit befuddled by all this. I couldn't see that Jesus would really care. I went so far as to consider for the first time that I might know something that the pastor didn't. But as I said, I was a church girl, and that was the limit of my rebellious thought. I wanted to be a good Lutheran. I even wanted to be a Lutheran deaconess, since I couldn't be a nun, which sounded more rigorous and self-sacrificing. The stories of martyrs resonated with me.

It was a circuitous route, but through the changes in women's rights during the seventies, I ended up not a deaconess but a fully ordained pastor about forty years later. And here I was with questions again. How would I spend these unexpected ten days away from work and home with the space to explore and reflect on them in depth? I turned quite naturally yet ironically toward what I was resisting—the church. I discovered I could buy a packet of tickets to tour the historic churches—*le chiesa storiche*—in Verona while my friend went to work.

One cathedral a day. I couldn't really take in more than one. Even with great intention and awareness, the creative excesses were numbing. There was no dull corner or bare wall. Each was a frenzy of fading frescoes, soaring pillars, Romanesque and Gothic arches, Renaissance paintings, gilded altars, inlaid marble floors, and ornately carved railings, spindles, and confessionals. The main doors were high and heavy, inlaid with copper carvings and bearing massive handles, the thick wood aching with memories and the touch of the penitent. The echoes of history made it even harder to stay present to what was bombarding the eyes; my mind would be trying to apprehend the centuries of time I was seeing—and I could get only so far before faltering. I was weighed down by the thickness of the paint as I tried to understand how the artist had been inspired, thinking I should feel more and feel it more deeply. I tried to meditate, but the ancient stones held the cold like a grip and soon I shivered, unable to concentrate on anything but my tingling fingers and arms. I gazed at the silver face masks on the wall of what I assumed were former cardinals and bishops. Tombs of church hierarchy were embedded in the floor as well. I felt nothing, even in my most charitable mood. I went to the center of the sanctuary where the cross was formed by the intersection of the east–west nave with the north–south transepts. I thought perhaps here I would get the clarity I needed; here I would integrate what the faith-inspired artistry was trying desperately to tell me, here at the center of the cross. But for all my earnest trying, I felt nothing—only inadequacy for the task. What was keeping me from making a deeper connection?

On the fourth day of church visiting, I was in the Duomo, named the Catedral Santa Maria Matricolare—the grand cathedral of Verona. When I entered, a harpist was practicing near the altar, the music from the strings reverberating in the space and lifting my heart. Maybe I would feel something here. Still listening, I wandered the perimeter of the sanctuary, a little lost in the immense grandeur, wondering if one person could find belonging here, when suddenly a middle-aged woman came up to me in great excitement, her red hair flying as her hands tried to paint her words. At first I thought I must be violating some rule of the cathedral or there was some sin apparent just in being American, but her face was alight and those beautiful Italian words that swirled around me weren't scolding. Even when I said, "no capiche," an Americanized version of "I don't understand," she continued her long speech to me, unable to contain herself. She kept pointing to the wall near the side corner of the sanctuary and repeating, "Bella, bella, bella! Magnifique!" I realized then she wanted to share something with me, but I saw nothing remarkable about that wall.

Taking me by the hand, she led me, and I saw then it was a door, so dark it was almost black. When I pushed it open, it led down a set of stairs with light at the end. Seeing that I understood now, she looked entirely pleased, as if she had fulfilled some contract. I was so humbled by her help and her simple desire to share this secret, but I couldn't tell her in words. Instead we beamed at each other and then clasped each other's hands as if sharing a deep bond. Then she turned and left as rapidly as she arrived. I took a breath and went back through the swinging door, only wide enough for one person to pass through. Evidently, I was to go on alone.

I started down rose-colored stone steps. At the first turn, I was surprised to find the floor dug and exposed down another fifteen feet. A man and a woman scurried on narrow scaffolding, brushing stone, nearly white with the dust of their work, yet intent. When I looked at them, I thought, "They are doing the thing they were meant to do." Through broken English, I learned they were uncovering the foundations of the Duomo, perhaps the first church to be built on that site in the fourth century. And below that, an ancient spa. They were intense but intent, hurrying, yet not with a need to get done, only a desire to unwrap the treasure further. I watched for a while, willing myself to imagine the earth and people here in ancient time. An old, old memory stirred in the dirt, and I settled for awe.

I followed the passageway toward a door of light. And now I could see more fully the buried treasure. It was another sanctuary under the one where I had just wandered! But this one was so simple. The frescoes here were pale reds and greens—and they seemed to be in the process of being absorbed by the walls or peering out at me through a fine veil. The altar was a simple slab; a single plain wooden cross hung over it. There were many benches, all surrounding the real centerpiece of this place—the huge marble baptistery—big enough for ten people to stand inside, probably the site of the original spa and artesian well. Around its three-foot façade, the figures of the Bible paraded, somehow seeming to move yet encased in stone. I sat for a while in a little side portico before a picture of Mother Mary, her robe outstretched and protecting a crowd of people pressing close to her. Above me, one floor up, lay the thick marble pillars, the soaring arches filled with the faces of angels, and the golden candlesticks ten feet high. But here it was the color of the earth, and there was a contented silence. A womb, I thought. The womb of Mary.

The history of patriarchy in the church had always rankled me. In fact, it was one of the reasons I decided to be ordained, to break into

The wide arms of the Feminine Divine

the male ranks of clergy. At my ordination, I named the women present who had wanted to be pastors but weren't allowed to go to seminary in their generation. One of them was on the same plane I was when I flew down to my first semester of seminary. She saw me and came forward, took my hand and said, "Go do it for us."

The Duomo flaunted the lack of the feminine in my face. All those popes and cardinals in relief. All those tombs of male church officials from centuries past dug into the floor. Then this contrast of the simple and feminine sense of the original church, anchored near water and needing little else. I needed to face my resentment and reactivity about patriarchy and be honest about it. So many of my male clergy colleagues were anything but patriarchal. Yet the religion as a whole was steeped in it. Men wrote the Bible. Men wrote the Apostles' Creed. Men decided the liturgy. Men were "most like Jesus." And on and on. I let myself just feel what I was feeling. It was buried, but this was part of the soul wound. Being a female in leadership in the Christian Church was still frowned upon by most denominations. Most were still putting women in second place. It was good to feel the sadness of it—the repression of the Divine Feminine. I sat in the sun of a nearby restaurant and restored myself with a magnificent caprese salad and a glass of Prosecco.

I wasn't sure I wanted to visit any more medieval churches. Maybe I had learned what I was to learn. But there is a part of me that finishes the list. The next day I was again wandering around the aisles of Chiesa di Santa Anastasia, studying my tourist pamphlet that said at the top, "A Thousand Years of Faith." I went slowly from one painting to another, from one sculpture to tomb, asking for these things to open me to the faith that formed the foundations of all that I saw. But nothing had changed; it felt mostly cold and unmoving. The altar was surrounded by carvings of all the saints, the black worn confessionals with little red cushions lined the walls, and I formed my own confession, wondering if I could believe that all be forgiven by a repetition of Hail Marys—and did the priests themselves believe it?

I entered a small alcove to escape the expanse of the ceilings and the faces of saints and popes crushing down on me. I decided to kneel to pray. The kneeler was pushed behind some chairs and against a small side door. I stood there intrigued by the door and wondering what was behind it when a small white-haired woman appeared at my side talking in Italian and wanting me to understand something. Again, I thought I had violated something deemed sacred—perhaps she was worried that I was going to open the door, as I had, in fact, wanted to pull the handle. But I soon realized she was assisting me in moving the kneeler in front of the small altar, and she wasn't warning me at all. The look on her face was of shining happiness. After she saw that my kneeler was in place, she seemed satisfied and content like the red-haired woman in the Duomo. She knelt beside me on her own kneeler, and for a while, we prayed there together. When I looked over at her, she was smiling, as if it were a great pleasure to be with me. I looked at the small door and wondered what was behind it. But slowly I was more intrigued by the mystery of the woman beside me, who could take so much joy in praying with me, without knowing me or understanding me. Just that I was a fellow believer in resurrection. The painting above the altar loomed over us; Mary smiling, holding the fat baby Jesus. The smile was the same as that of the woman kneeling beside me. The welcome of Mary. The Divine Feminine may have been repressed and controlled in ages past, but it was still alive and well here in this small church. And there was still faith. I felt consoled.

Later that week, I took a bus trip up to Lake Garda and out to a small town at the end of long tip of land that extended into that sea. I loved the way it sounded as it is said, *Sirmione* (Sear-me-o-nay). The bus dropped me off just yards away from the drawbridge over the castle moat where swans fed and small boats bobbed at the shoreline. Once over the bridge, I was in the old town and narrow streets of the ancient village, inhabited in the first century BCE by the Roman poet Catullo. I walked the ruins of his villa in the morning, pinching myself just to be sure I was really here and awake, strolling through the olive orchard, full of the first small daisies and violets of spring. The lake spilled out on three sides around me as I became a woman of ancient Rome, imagining myself in flowing white gowns, embroidered in gold.

After a long lunch in the café, I found the village church, Santa Maria Maggiore, and settled in by a long window on the side to sit and wait. It was the only place where light flowed in when the doors at the back were closed.

One other person shared the church with me, an older woman sitting quietly in the front pew. A beautiful iron tree of twelve burning candles stood at the front of the nave. A small slot for donations opened on the table just in front of it. I sat three rows back from the woman and tried to translate the words on the altar cloth: La Verita vi fara Liberi. Later she rose carefully and approached the large carving of Jesus on the cross that stood beside the candles. She stood still for a long while at the crucifix, just looking—and then she kissed the tips of her fingers and touched them to the wounds of Jesus. She caressed his face and his side, his legs and his feet in a way that I wasn't sure she thought of him as Son of God or as Lover. She sat back down and held me there in her authentic and deep silence. A voice in me murmured something condescending about her simple, sentimental believing, but another aching voice whispered, *If I could have that faith.*

Sometime in the silence, people entered beside me. I looked up surprised. Then I realized what I thought was a window was really a plastic swinging door. I heard it close, "whap, whap, whap," each time someone entered during the then noon hour. It was distracting and irritating until I shifted into asking the question, *"Why am I noticing this?"* The noise of the constant opening and closing repeated itself again and again. And I began to wonder if God was telling me that my journey ahead would not be closing a door behind me; it would be a swinging door, where I went back and forth from the old to the new in my disciplines, my theology, my practices of faith, and in my understanding of the role of men and women in the church. I felt an ease in my soul. Maybe I would not have to choose whether to stay in the church or not. Nor would I need to play a role to stay in the church. An idea introduced itself to me: *The church needs you to be who you are.*

I closed my eyes. The noon visitors waned. There was silence again, full and rich silence. When I opened my eyes, the woman was lighting a candle. I let my eyes drift to above the altar again, to Mary, the Queen of Heaven, wearing a gold crown and magnificent robe. She seemed too distant and holy to be the Mary that spoke to me. Had the church made her so holy, she was no longer human? Was she too feminine to be trusted as she was? Would she ask questions about authority? Better to have her behind glass where she's revered but not heard?

When my eyes slid back to the altar cloth, I realized I did know what the words said—*The truth shall set you free.*

Despite the fact that it was my desire as a teen, it wasn't easy for me to become a pastor. I was a church girl but not so much a church woman. The churches of Verona hammered me with my fears of patriarchy, the male image of God, the emphasis of suffering and hell rather than birth or resurrection, and the need for huge edifices and plaques and tombs and spires. Was it consecration or competition? Extolling God or exacting ego? How did this fit with a God who chose to come to earth a baby, be born in a barn, and live as a poor carpenter? In my most cynical moment, I wondered if the church—that is, the popes and the patriarchy who taught that Mary Magdalene was a whore (despite the fact the Scripture didn't say that)—made Mary, the mother of Jesus, an unrealistic model for women. Yet her power and her truth were there.

When I remember those three women in those three churches, I saw that I needed the balance of these women to wake me to the fact that the essence of the Holy is glorious and yet hidden. The greatest truths come not in logic but in faith. The feminine wisdom, the old Sophia spoken of in the Old Testament, joined with Mary to ground the church into the earth as its spires ascend to heaven. Women's wisdom is needed to balance the wisdom of men or the church will not be whole. Three Wise Women came bearing me gifts; elder women, full of excitement about the subterranean mysteries of God—simplicity, compassion, and communion—in the midst of light and suffering. And always, Mother Mary there with her robe open to hold in the seekers. Each story associated with a small hidden door, just waiting to be opened.

I was sensing something new about my own spiritual journey as a woman then. My understanding deepened not with answers but with more questions. I was a woman speaking the language of the patriarchal church, walking in a role prescribed by generations of men. It doesn't easily shift. And I discovered the person most resistant to accepting my new power and possibility in the role was myself. I was constantly in doubt of what I was preaching. Was it true? Would it offend? Should it offend more? Should I act more in control to give others assurance or be more vulnerable so others could do so as well? My own history of how a woman should look and act clawed at me. The church's suspicion of women's way of knowing and leading were still markers on my cells no matter how much my heart rejected it.

I had so long struggled with words like *sanctification, salvation*, or *sin* that are standard fare in church language. Even if I understood the theological basis of the words and the truth that undergirded them, they felt as if they had lost their original meaning in the ages of liturgical repetition. I even held back at the usual ending to prayer, "in the name of Jesus Christ, our Lord and Savior. Amen." *Lord and Savior* were not the words for the deep connection I felt in Christ's energy. Christ as King of Kings, Christ as the Sacrificial Lamb, Christ as Final Sacrifice were syllables in my mouth, not stirrings from the faith in my heart. What had changed? Why were the cornerstones of my former faith now shifting sand? And why now when I had spent so much time and real suffering to make the dream of becoming pastor a reality?

At a funeral of a dear friend where I helped preside, I heard myself saying things in words that felt dead to me as well. "Washed in the blood of Christ." The words were not the words of my truth. Suddenly my stole and cross felt heavy, and inside I heard a whisper, *I will not do this again.*

Walking the streets of Verona, I was torn by the paradox of loving the church and dying inside of it. My heart felt broken by the commitment I had made out of love that now felt like duty. I felt like the betrayer and the betrayed. How could the Spirit have led me into this? Or had I been fooling myself all along and done it all out of egoic motivations? Would I have to leave the church? Or would I find the compromise that I felt in the church in Sirmione? I was getting clarity, and it began in the sanctuaries of Italy, the landscape of love.

I didn't know at the time that my walking in the churches of Verona and Sirmione and along the winding streets that connected them was a pilgrimage. Only now do I see how all the elements of transformation were there—the longing to understand my place as a woman in church, the physical fatigue of walking for hours, the intense and unending contemplation. Verona has a walking trail along the top of the ancient wall of the original city. I remember ambling along it, sick with a bad cold, feeling vulnerable and unsteady, wondering if I might slip off the wall. The connection and the disconnection with the Holy. And yet in the midst of all the confusion was what veteran pilgrim and author Phil Cousineau called in *The Art of Pilgrimage* the "eruption of the Divine."

Near the end of my time in Verona, I was walking back with my friend to our hotel when we got caught up in a stream of people, hurrying along to some destination. Where were they all going? Our curiosity prompted us to follow along as rain started to pelt down with a fury. We soon realized we were headed to a side door of the great cathedral. Inside we were crowded into a small lower chapel, pressed together so all could come in. It truly seemed like a place to find sanctuary. Older women (who all had dyed red hair), young men in corporate suits holding toddlers around their necks, teens who were bouncing on their toes with headphones slung around their necks jostled together. It was as if everyone from the town was represented there. The priest was young and tall, and in the light of the single large candle behind him, he seemed to glow golden. Wet and pressed together, the room was warm and steamy.

I didn't understand anything the priest was saying, but I felt his benevolence. The whole crowd seemed to lean toward him, yearning. He walked among us, blessing everyone, passing out the Eucharist. I cannot claim what happened in those moments, but a Presence filled the room. All seemed right with the world. I could love every person standing there. I felt I was experiencing what Christ called *koinonia*—the fellowship of the church. Even my friend, who when asked about church, would say, "I'm not too affected," turned to me and said, "It's enough to make you believe." My final church in Verona would remind me of the purity of what could be in this gathering we call church.

It was this that in its essence had always called me to church; the possibility that a group of imperfect humans yearning to return to the purity of their being would try together to drop the masks. And by grace, be in union with the Mystery that created them.

The Camino loomed in my mind as I walked in Verona. It was still a year away, but my inner compass was turned to it. I wrote in my journal while I was there:

> I am more sensitive to change and environment than I realize. This trip showed me this; it has made me wonder about doing the Camino. Could I really do it with all these headaches, that day of vertigo, the neck pain and back pain? The inability to sleep through someone snoring? I know that is part of the journey—moving past discomfort and fear. I guess I'll know when the time comes.

I returned to the church I was serving in Anchorage, sensing into all I had experienced, and waited to see how my soul would fare. Could I find a way of being my true self and staying in this call? Would I see how to hold other's hearts while holding mine? But instead of creating something different, the busyness only increased. The senior pastor of the church resigned to become bishop, and suddenly I was the senior pastor with even more duties. The congregation was great, but with its many members, there was simply a lot to manage. I officiated at seven funerals that summer, negotiated the demands of the Neighborhood Drop-In Center for kids and listened to divided opinions on social issues. As I felt a deep melancholy setting in, I began to wonder if God was making it plain to me; it's time to leave.

Six months after my return from Verona, I resigned my position, not so much out of clarity but out of necessity for my health. I left with gratitude for all I learned and accomplished, the friendships made, and the faith that had been shared. But deep remorse jangled, too, feeling I had somehow failed.

I entered another six months of inner wandering. I was back in a dark womb, desperately hoping I was being reformed and remade. I felt lost at times, purposeless, perhaps a fraud, both a victim and the perpetrator of that crime of forgetting one's true self. It was a time of tortured waiting; a huge void opened now that work could not fill the ache inside. I took long walks in the woods that edged the glacial river close to my home. Watching it flow with such certainty down to the ocean, knowing exactly where it was going; that was the clarity I so wanted. How would I satisfy this yearning if not in the tradition of the church?

Looking back at my journal entries, I remember that I threw myself into reading books about spiritual development. I began having sessions with a spiritual intuitive. I saw my spiritual director. I escaped with camping in wilderness. I concocted exotic recipes in my kitchen. I meditated every day. I traveled to the Philippines for three weeks with friends to visit their son in the Peace Corps. I went to retreats, and I led retreats at Stillpoint in Halibut Cove, Alaska. It was my new version of workaholism, but the awareness was growing. I wrote this quote from James Hillman at the front of my journal at that time: "You have to give up the life you have to get the life that's waiting for you." And above it, that quote from Jesus himself: "In order to save your life, you must lose it."

As I kept pondering the Camino, I would reread the Scripture that Joyce Rupp spoke about during that very retreat that started my desire to go on pilgrimage; it hearkened back to those hidden doors in Verona: "There is a door opening for you." I hoped it was true.

Another interesting door on the streets of Verona

May you travel in an awakened way,
gathered wisely into your inner ground,
that you may not waste the invitations
which wait along the way.

JOHN O'DONOHUE

Chapter 3

Taking the First Steps

It was late in the fall of 2006 when Steve and I finally began to plan to walk the Camino Frances. I began my research on the Internet about how to prepare for a journey of five hundred miles. I joined a forum of former travelers to hear their tips and their tales. I ordered a detailed guidebook that most of them recommended called *A Pilgrim's Guide to the Camino de Santiago* by John Brierley. He described it as "a practical and mystical manual for the modern-day pilgrim." The combination of practical and mystical described me. This guidebook would follow the Camino Frances route from St. Jean Pied Pont in France to Santiago, Spain—the destination of the Camino no matter what route you took. We knew we didn't want to miss summer in Alaska, and April and early May are still chilly here. From an Internet search, it looked as if the temperatures in Spain would be in the sixties during those months, a temperature perfect for hiking.

We had about six months to prepare. The first thing I did was purchase all the CDs and books used in the beginning Spanish class at the local university and hired a tutor to assist me in having some working Spanish for the trip. She advised me to watch Spanish soap operas on TV. "That's how immigrants often learn our language," she said. And although we had always been walkers, Steve and I began to step up our distance, particularly two months prior to travel, walking three to four hours at a time. I reasoned that we would walk in the morning on the pilgrimage, have a long lunch, and then walk again in the afternoon, making time for a good rest.

As the time got closer, I started to pack. Or mostly pack, weigh my bag, and then unpack. Our packs would be our friends, snack bars, first-aid stations, clothes closets, libraries, and back rests for this trip.

We wanted to follow the ancient rules of the pilgrimage as closely as possible, and one of those was to carry only 10 percent of your body weight on your back. That would mean thirteen pounds for me and sixteen pounds for Steve. It seemed a daunting task. I bought the lightest backpack available at REI. Two pounds. I packed one change of pants, shirt, and underwear and socks. I added a fleece jacket and raingear, trimmed-down toiletries, a pair of flip-flops for the evenings, a water bottle, a flashlight, hat and gloves, a tiny camera, sunglasses, and, as any good Alaskan would, duct tape. Twelve pounds. That left only a pound for carrying food during the day—and my water bottle wasn't full yet. For the first time in my life, I wished I weighed more, so I could carry more! Steve would have to carry the guidebook.

"Trust that all else will be provided," says the guidebook.

"Yes," said a practical friend, "*and* take your ATM card."

I remember the early morning we left for the airport, checking our backpacks over and over just one more time, asking several times if we had packed this and that until we were driving each other a little crazy. I took a final gulp as we walked out the door, knowing we weren't returning for six weeks.

We traveled eighteen hours by plane from Anchorage to Madrid, where we waited six hours to catch a train, which took us north for three more hours to Pamplona. We weren't even sure if we could find a ride to St. Jean Pied Pont once we arrived. The station master in Pamplona wasn't interested in my questions about getting to St. Jean but pointed outside and said, "Taxi." Sure enough there were two other travelers intent on walking the Camino. Using some sign language, we agreed to share the cab and stuffed ourselves and our gear in the small car. As the taxi wound its way up the steep road over the Pyrenees,

I realized I would be climbing these very mountains in the opposite way in the morning.

The taxi dumped us off in the center of town. Excitement and apprehension welled up as we trudged up the Rue de Citadelle to the pilgrim office. There is a long tradition on the Camino Frances that the pilgrim must have a pilgrim passport before embarking. The passport is then stamped at each stop along the way to prove one has made the journey. We had read in our guidebook that to get one in St. Jean Pied de Pont, where we would set forth, one must go to Mme. de Brill, who would or would not approve your journey. She would want to know, Why? Reading how contrary, demanding, and reluctant she might be to give out the passport if the answer was not to her liking, I tried to prepare my answer. Would "I had this dream" be sufficient?

It was almost a disappointment when there was no interrogation or doubtful glance of an old woman who would certify me. In the past few years, that had all changed. The Camino passport could be received by simply paying a small fee and filling out paperwork. The only thing that came close to Mme. de Brill's interrogation was the question on the form that asked: "Reason for pilgrimage: Religious? Spiritual? Cultural? Sport?" I realized I wanted to tell them why. I wanted to name the yearning. I wanted them to see in me the strength and faith and call to walk the five hundred miles (804 kilometers) ahead.

The volunteers at the office were patient and kind. They spoke many languages and weren't annoyed by all the anxious questions being asked on all sides. "Is it safe to cross the Pyrenees tomorrow?" "We've heard there was snow last week and someone got lost and died?" "Will the fog roll in tomorrow?" "Will we lose our way?" The man at the desk stamped our passports and gave us a chart of the elevations of the Camino, names of places where we could sleep for cheap as a *peregrino* (Spanish for pilgrim), and distances in kilometers between towns. He looked up and said simply, "Tomorrow will be a good day. It will be fine. Do not worry. Many people do this. You will too."

It was already late in the day when we left the pilgrim office, anxious for a little food and a good bed. As we wandered the streets, we saw the sign for the *albergue*, basically a bunkhouse for peregrinos that is cheap, four to seven euros, if you have a pilgrim passport. But it was crowded and noisy and we wanted to recover from the long trip to get here. So we began asking at hostels—cheaper accommodations but with private rooms—and inns, even more expensive. We didn't realize then that we really didn't have a choice. Every accommodation in the town was full. As would happen often on this trip, village folks must have recognized our plight as we stood at an intersection near the pilgrim office, trying to read a map and looking lost. Three or four villagers surrounded us, confirmed we needed a place to sleep, and assured us they would help. One of them made a phone call, and we assumed by their gestures that a place had been found. Soon a private car appeared, and we were whisked away through winding streets, across the River Nive running through town, and up a steep hill to a little hotel. A huge church surrounded by gravestones rose up from across the street, and I noticed that the lights hit the top of one marker so that it projected a shadow of a huge cross upon the church wall.

That first night was like a foreshadowing of the uncertainties I would face on the Camino. We were surrounded by languages we couldn't understand. Literally no one was speaking English—a delicious but tiring venture into being understood. Our credit card didn't work at the restaurant that night. In hindsight, I think the owner wanted cash instead. I went to the ATM across the street to get money, but my debit card didn't work. I felt my stomach tighten in fear. Why wasn't it working? I had planned on this little card to provide all the cash we would need on the trip. We rushed to another ATM down the street where to my greater than great relief, it happily spit out euros. How wonderful to have money—how fragile its security.

I would also know the same fatigue every day of the journey—bone tired and aching, the pains shifting to different parts of my body. And

like this first night, I often would not know where or if I would find a
place to sleep each night due to the numbers of pilgrims. But if I knew
anything, it was the sense that my feet upon those cobblestones of the
Rue de Citadelle were walking on the faith and intention of thousands
before me. And I did know the earth beneath my feet. It pulled on me
deeply and fiercely, grounding me with each step.

A decision to walk the Camino may have had a vague unnamed
motivation for many of us, but the man at the pilgrim office said over
90 percent of the peregrinos walking that year marked on the form that
they had a religious or spiritual reason for walking. As I walked and
talked with fellow pilgrims, I learned there were many different spiritual and religious reasons as well. For a few, it was the traditional belief
that God would reward them for doing this penance; but for most, that
theology didn't work anymore. Many were walking in hopes that the
silence and purging of possessions would help them find peace of mind,
more clarity, or healing from grief. Others felt that simply walking on
the *ley* lines of the Camino would stir up good energy and they would
connect with themselves and others in a more transcendent way. Some
felt the many chapels, crosses, and cathedrals would turn their heart to
God, and that God in turn would be closer. For most, the Camino was
a journey where they hoped they would encounter a new, even transformative, way of living a life full of meaning. I think there is a deep
restlessness in all pilgrims, and that is why they walk. Perhaps it is that
deep longing—and paradoxically deep fear—of surrendering all to God,
not knowing what that means.

The tradition of the pilgrimage of the Camino de Santiago calls forth
noble ideals and a humble spirit. When I read the following inscription
on the outside of one of the albergues, it seemed to me like the Ten
Commandments of the Camino pilgrim. Some of them pleased me,
some challenged me, and some seemed quaint. I wrote them down in
my journal though and as the days wore on, I would reference them now
and then, understanding more of their wisdom.

1. The Camino de Santiago is not a marathon.

2. The authentic camino is the one going on inside each one.

3. Optimism, and happiness, sincerity and sympathy are qualities of an authentic pilgrim.

4. The most important luggage that a pilgrim carries is an attitude of seeking.

5. The starting point of the camino is to not have prejudices for anyone.

6. The camino is an opportunity for a constant encounter of self in the other.

7. Always have the eyes to recognize beauty and art.

8. During the walking, nothing you encounter is ever the same to you.

9. Respect nature, and you can learn much.

10. St. James, guide and give good fortune to this pilgrim.

We began our journey the next morning at the cathedral, standing at the back of a cold and dark sanctuary where small candles flickered in front of the statues of Mary. We stood in silence, knowing simply that we didn't know what was ahead or if we would make it. We said a prayer there in the darkness that we would say every morning of our journey to Santiago:

Lord, we thank you for this day. Give us courage and strength as we walk upon the way. Open us to your freedom and your grace; help us to see you in another pilgrim's face. Protect us from all that is not of you, yet open my heart to love as you would do. Bless this earth that gives us life this day and be with those for whom we pray. Amen.

We were armed with our Brierley guidebook and had studied the first day carefully. The author suggested a schedule of roughly 24 kilometers (15 miles) a day which would take thirty-four days to get to Santiago with two rest days. We had allowed another week to get back to Madrid just in case things didn't go as smoothly as his agenda. The guidebook allowed space each day as a place to journal my reflections. This structure, so different from my prior journeys, created our experience, day by day by day. And so it began.

Day 1. St. Jean de Pied Pont to Roncesvalles: 24.8 km; adjusted for climb: 31.7 km (19.8 miles) (Note: adjusted for climb acknowledges that more distance is covered when going up and over rather than walking on a flat path.)

It was springtime, April 25, 2007. There had been snow in the Pyrenees two weeks prior. But the temperature was in the fifties that morning. When I looked up at the mountains, the highest peaks were in clouds and a mist moved in and around the valley. I could feel the bursting eagerness to start, but there would be no place to stop for lunch on this first stretch. So we waited for shops to open and to have that particular pleasure of buying crusty baguettes, soft French cheeses, yellow apples, and of course, chocolate. A stop to buy a knife in another shop. A stop to fill our water bottles. A deep breath. At last.

There was an archway near the river that marked the beginning of our five-hundred-mile journey, Porte St. Jacques. The earlier dream began to have a specific road, smell, view, and incline. There was our first blue-and-yellow scallop shell sign to mark the way. We were on the Camino at last. It was like a giant keyhole, opening a door to an inner adventure that hummed with expectation and mystery.

It was humbling to remember that the original pilgrims went with so little and truly depended for their lives, not just their comfort, on the

The beginning of our pilgrimage on the Rue de Citadelle

hospitality of the Camino. In the Middle Ages, they left with a staff, a gourd for water, and their long woolen clothes for warmth. I had walked many miles in the two months before the trip to ready, getting up to 10 to 12 miles a day. I had wondered if my back would allow me to walk the whole way, and then just the day before leaving my knee was acting up. Yet they seemed such small ailments when I remembered the history of pilgrims desperately ill, walking the Camino in hopes of a miracle cure, hoping this act of faith would call on the mercy of God. The numerous hospitals and hospices, mostly now in ruins, bore a steady reminder of the severity of the journey of early pilgrims and how many had died before reaching Santiago. If my back hurt, I could get someone to call a taxi.

At the end of the first day we had climbed about forty-five hundred feet through the rolling hills of the Pyrenees, past bucolic scenes of barns and sheep grazing beside early spring flowers. Griffin vultures soared overhead, and beautiful golden horses wandered the high country with bells on their necks. Near the top the mist settled in, and we passed and were passed by our fellow pilgrims either on foot or on bikes. We began to hear the byword of the pilgrimage—*Buen Camino!* (Good journey!) The terrain grew rocky, and we left the road to follow a narrow footpath up through huge boulders, and then finally we were at the pass. We were on the road that Napoleon's troops followed as they moved to conquer the region. The legends said that the troops must walk 50 kilometers a day. I would walk 31 kilometers by day's end and was fairly sure I couldn't take another step, let alone 20 kilometers more by the time we reached Roncesvalles, an old monastery that would be our first albergue of the journey. By the time I collapsed in the bunk, I was exhausted both from mental and physical fatigue. But my back and my knee had been fine.

Three long rows of iron bunkbeds holding 120 peregrinos filled the old stone hall of the monastery. The host arranged for Steve and me to have top bunks beside each other. It was so quiet considering all the people getting ready for bed. Packs rustled and people changed clothes. A hushed murmur filled the hall, and we nodded to each other with small smiles.

I thought I might have trouble falling asleep with so many people around me, a strange bed, and a flat pillow, but I fell asleep as my eyes closed. In the middle of the night, I awoke, seeing the shadows of the

The first shrine on our ascent of the Pyrenees

Gothic arches reflected on the walls. I took out my earplugs just to hear the sounds of the other pilgrims sleeping. As I heard the whispers of breathing in and breathing out and watched the flickering shadows on the arches, there was a moment of deep peace, of wide community, of transcendent connection that overwhelmed me. I had never been so grateful for a narrow bed with a thin mattress.

Confessions: While appearing to take my time and walk "in a relaxed manner," I had been anxious about getting to the first stop. And when we arrived, there was some trouble finding us beds. *Why had we tarried and laid in the sun when we should have gotten here sooner?* And I already was judging my fellow pilgrims for knocking loudly and yelling (in German) on the shower door because they thought my three-minute shower was too long. I was expecting kindness and support from all the other pilgrims. Already I had an idea of the Camino with some kind of perfection. And of my fellow travelers as well. And of myself.

Day 2. Roncesvalles to Zubiri: 22.2 km; adjusted for climb: 23.5 km (14.7 miles)

At six the next morning, the booming baritone of one of the hosts woke us by singing, "Hallelujah, hallelujah, hallelujah, hallelujah!" As I would every morning for the next five weeks, I cautiously moved my body, checking to see how it had fared after the long hike of yesterday. I eased down from the top bunk to the floor amid a mass of people packing their packs and dressing. Early on I realized Europeans have far less modesty than most Americans, and far less need to smell good.

We perched on a stone wall outside the albergue eating yogurt. It was still dark when we began our walk to the next small town, Burguete, where we had the first of many *bocadillos* at an outdoor café.

Bocadillos are the mainstay of pilgrims, as rarely would we be on the eating schedule of the majority of Spain. Bocadillos are sandwiches with usually three main choices: cheese, ham, or eggs (no butter, no mayo, no lettuce). My first bocadillo was a huge omelette folded inside a fresh, crusty baguette. As we ate, I read from our guidebook that Ernest Hemingway had loved this town and spent much time here.

Outside the church next door, we said our morning prayer again. Since we did not stay in any place for more than one night, the sameness of this prayer gave us a feeling of home. The landscape here was so foreign to us, so embedded with signs of centuries of civilization on all sides; in Alaska, there are still places you can walk for days and not see another person or sign of humankind.

I couldn't find wilderness in Spain. Perhaps that is why we felt homesick at times. Just minutes from my back door in Alaska, a wide glacial river flows down Eagle River valley past my home, and I can often fit my hand into the imprint of grizzly tracks when I walk on its banks of gray silt. Moose browse in the woods in my backyard. Lynx prowl, and eagles soar overhead.

The top of the Pyrenees did have a wild feeling where I could imagine fierce Basque fighters once crouched behind those huge boulders, protecting their turf, but I couldn't call it wilderness. We were never out of sight of markers or fences or domesticated animals. There did not seem to be a place I could name as "untamed," and that is my best definition of wilderness. I would not find the wilderness I know in Alaska on this Camino. But I would find an interior wilderness—a place of beauty and beasts, a place of silence and struggle.

That second morning I was strolling through farms and pastures, vast forests of beech trees and purple crocus, telling myself over and over, *You are walking the Camino de Santiago. This is it. You are in Spain. Don't miss it. Pay attention.* The journey was mostly downhill that day. We began to meet other pilgrims, some who would be our companions off and on until the end. The most interesting that day were two young women pushing a carriage and carrying a baby of three months in a sling. We assumed they were day trippers from the last town out for exercise. But we would learn eventually that this was a young mother, with the help of a girlfriend, who was walking her baby to Santiago to be baptized in the cathedral there. She would be joined by many other young men and women as they walked along until there was a cadre of ten to twelve from Italy, Ireland, Australia, and Canada who helped her carry the baby and push the load. Over the next five weeks, we could even see the changes in little Luke as we bumped into him and his mother, usually breastfeeding outside a café. In contrast, an old woman came to the window of her home as we passed by and blessed us with her hands and the steady gaze of her eyes. She was not walking with us bodily, but I knew she sent her spirit with us where her old limbs would not take her. I wondered if she had once walked to Santiago.

That afternoon at the next albergue in Zubiri we again realized there was a dearth of beds available but finally found two upper bunks in one of the dorms where a German woman seemed intent on taking over as the boss of bed assignments. We pretended not to understand and took the bunks we wanted. Later pilgrims would sleep on the floor in the gymnasium next door.

Confessions: I am getting a little irritated with the Germans. And what did fifth commandment of the Camino say? *The starting point of the camino is to not have prejudices for anyone.* Do I already need to go back to the starting point? Also, I don't want to stop to give my feet a rest like I know I should. I didn't know it would bother me so much to have people pass me.

Day 3. Zubiri to Pamplona: 21.9 km; adjusted for climb: 23.8 km (14.8 miles)

We walked on to Pamplona the next day, originally thinking we'd stroll right through this city of two hundred thousand. We assumed it would be too jarring after the rural landscapes. But we loved it. We were thrilled to see the arches of old Roman bridges and then the massive castle walls on the hill, imagining the knights and princesses, the warriors and the wars that had taken place on this soil. It was hot and sunny, and new spring flowers were competing for our attention on all sides. Pamplona— the city of Hemingway and the running of the bulls, sprawling parks and greens, friendly people, and Steve's first sighting of a drawbridge. But the albergue was full. We walked in circles until finally finding a bare room in a side hotel where we pushed a button on an indistinct gray wall to find admittance.

Confessions: I had already lost my faith in the adage, "Trust and you will always have a place to sleep at night." Maybe or maybe not. All the lodgings weren't yet open in the season, and the race to the next albergue was getting quietly more competitive. Or was that just me? What was that commandment? *The Camino is not a marathon.*

Happy are those who trust you
And merge their will in your will.

PSALM 84

Chapter 4

And Then There's the Trust Issue

In Karen Armstrong's memoir about leaving the convent, *The Spiral Staircase,* she writes of a conundrum: "My life had kept changing but at the same time, I constantly found myself revolving round and round the same themes, the same issues, and even repeating the same mistakes." Whenever I go back and read my old journals, I'm always a little chagrined; like Armstrong, it seems the issues I was struggling with then—that I thought I had recognized, understood, and changed in my life—are the same ones still on my plate.

Aware I was hurrying each day on the Camino to get to the next albergue to find a bed, it was discouraging to see how soon I lost trust that God will provide on the Camino. I really thought I had learned this lesson of basic trust in whatever arises. I couldn't count the number of times that help arrived, the right person showed up, the right book fell into my hands, or an unexpected check showed up in the mail. When I was just twenty-three years old, I learned this on my first long journey away from home. In hindsight, I now call that trip a pilgrimage as well.

I'm not sure I even knew what the word *pilgrimage* meant. I called it a grand adventure, a stretching of my wings, and, unconsciously, an escape. Looking back, however, it fits my definition of pilgrimage perfectly. It was my first wandering, the first journey of outer walking that would replicate my inner journey. It would be a journey that rose out of longing, and it was a walking path that would awaken my demons and challenged my way of being.

In the fall of 1974 I was nearing the end of what I thought would be my formal education, and I was tired. Tired of tests and schedules and course synopses and expectations and requirements. I would graduate in a month after my undergraduate work in psychology from Iowa State and two intense years of training at the Mayo School of Physical Therapy. It was time to make a decision. Where would I take my first real job as a physical therapist? And who would be with me? Would I stay single or commit to a long-term relationship, possibly marriage? I was restless and uneasy, not settled in any decision. I felt wild inside but without the ground to support it. I relied on the opinions and reflections of others to mark my outline and to color in my spaces. I could even sense at times that I was betraying myself in some way but not aware enough of that self to know what it was. When my best friend Julie suggested we wait to make all those decisions and take a three-month backpacking trip to Europe, I signed on without hesitation. Hearing of our trip, my sister Karen came, too, having just graduated from nursing school.

That was the time when many in their twenties read *Europe on $10 a Day*, bought a Eurail pass for $167 for three months, and took off across the Atlantic with nothing but a backpack, hiking shoes, and a book of American Express traveler's checks. I had no savings, but I could cash in some US savings bonds that my great-uncle had bought for me every year for Christmas as I was growing up. He was no longer alive then, but my father, on his behalf, was aghast.

"That money was to help you get started in the world," he said. "To make a down payment on a house or save to start a family. Not to go gallivanting off on some harebrained trip. Uncle Ed would be turning over in his grave."

I had always acquiesced to the strong will of my father. He, who had overcome abandonment at age eight and endured forced labor on the farm of Uncle Ed, was a man who only knew hard work as a way of life—and as a measure of his worth. Even though it was usually the sons who helped with the farmwork, his first four children were girls. So he decided we would learn to work as boys would. There were chores before and after school, and all day on Saturday. Our only time off was after church on Sunday till four o'clock. Then chores again. It was a big farm of a thousand acres and a lot of livestock. The work was never done. Dad was short on praise and long on criticism. There was no talking back. So my decision to stand up to him was a turning point.

Cashing in the $1,000 in bonds was really the start of this first long journey away from home. I had the courage to break a family rule, to stand up to my father and to the Midwest small-town culture of that day that would expect me to get a job within a few hours driving distance of the family farm. I knew my actions would raise a few eyebrows. I knew I was disappointing others. But that wild restlessness had some boldness in it. I was going to Europe without their approval.

I didn't have any intentional spiritual agenda for the trip, but I was already a seeker. I'd been raised to believe fundamentally that only Christians got to heaven, and even more exclusively that Lutherans had the most correct theology. And within Lutheranism, that the German Lutherans were more correct than the Swedish Lutherans. In a town of less than two thousand, there were two Lutheran churches.

That fundamentalism had been blown apart fairly quickly at college at Iowa State. It was my first multicultural experience. I had never met a Black person and certainly not people from other countries. There was a large contingency of students from Iran who were studying farming methods, and after getting to know some of them, I realized they were Muslim. They were devout, faithful, kind, and loving. "Now how is it that I am saved and they are not?" I thought. "Is it really true that I get to go to heaven just because I was born to Christians and they weren't?" In that instant I dropped the belief that there was one way to God. It was fascinating how the truth was so clear to me. Of course, it escalated as I continued in college, questioning all my beliefs and not finding certain answers. I never felt like I had lost my foundation of faith, but all the walls were being knocked down. This too was part of the complexion of the journey I was about to take to Europe.

We flew from Montreal to Amsterdam for $269 round-trip in late September. The price determined our entry point into Europe. From there we had vowed to follow the "wayless way," as Meister Eckhart, the German theologian and mystic, called it. "To allow room for surprise and improvisation is to begin the apprenticeship of learning the way that is no way."

With only ten dollars a day to live on, our lives took on a rhythm of exploring all day, then jumping on a train with crusty bread, rich cheese, and a bottle of wine to take us to the next destination. After being initiated to the wonders of Europe by the colorful and meandering canals of Amsterdam, we headed south along the Rhine River, marveling at seeing our first vineyards and castles, learning how to manage unfamiliar currency and languages, and finding our way to youth hostels tucked away in strange corners each night.

If one of the purposes of pilgrimage is to open our eyes, then mine must have looked stunned very often. Seeing how the United States and its citizens were viewed abroad at the time of the Vietnam War made me want to do what other backpacking Americans were doing—sew a Canadian patch on my backpack. I was so awed by the centuries-old history of the Western civilization there, I was left feeling as if America was a teenager in comparison. To see that Europeans could speak at least three to five languages humbled me who knew only one fluently—plus just enough German and French to ask for simple things but not able to understand the answer!

We often played cards on the train, and it was easy to find others who wanted to join in, even if they had no understanding of the rules. One particular card game stands out to me as we were playing hearts with a couple of young men from Turkey. At one point, one of them turned to me and said slowly and thoughtfully, "I think you laugh too much." I could have taken that many ways, but I felt the truth of what he was saying. How did this young man perceive that laughing covered up insecurity in me? How was he already so wise?

Somewhere along the Rhine River as we sat on the hard, wooden benches of yet another train station, I looked up and saw that a train was heading to Oslo, Norway: the land of my mother's ancestors. I was the child of a grandmother who still cooked lefse on top of a woodstove in Iowa; a grandmother who had explained to me how they banked the coals just right so the huge rounds of thin white bread would cook evenly without burning. I remembered the long, thin stick used for turning the rounds from one side to another—and the blue rosemaling on the end of it, slightly chipped now after years of use. Grandma Ruth was from the region of Norway where they made their lefse from just flour, water, butter, and salt. I would learn later that every valley actually had its own lefse recipe, just as it had its own particular costume for special events. The lefse rounds my grandmother made were cooked until they were dry and could be stored for weeks in an airtight box. Every holiday, she would take the rounds out of the box and lay them between cotton sackcloth. Then she'd take a shaker used only for this purpose and carefully wet the towels between each of the rounds. Too much and the lefse would become doughy. Too little and it would be dry. She would bend over her work as if preparing the bread for communion at church—as if it was sacred—as if it tied an ancient story to the simple act of eating. I could see her there, hunched over the counter, lips pursed, intent on checking the lefse as it softened. We would never interrupt her, or we'd get a sharp reprimand. But when it was just right, she would take out the round, smear it with butter, and sprinkle it with cinnamon and sugar. Then she would fold it into a long flat tube and cut it at an angle so the servings were like diamonds. At last we were allowed to take one from the carefully arranged plate and let the familiar taste of our heritage fill our bodies, stir our souls. My grandmother didn't speak Norwegian as it was discouraged when they immigrated to America. But if the lefse burned or tore in the turning, an exclamation of *Uff da* would explode from her lips.

I had grown up knowing the customs, the jewelry, the stories of trolls, and the pictures of fjords of Norway. Seeing Oslo on the train schedule that day called to me like a siren. Julie and Karen were willing to change plans, and we hopped on the next train north, taking with us the wines of the Mosel, the thick crusty bread of the local bakery, some soft stinky cheese that melted in my mouth, and because we were in Germany, a good chunk of sausage. If I wanted to explore my Norwegian roots, the time was now; it was the first of October and the weather was turning cold. Little did I know then, Karen and I would actually meet one of our ancestors there.

It was on this trip that we began to sense that there was a divine Presence that accompanied us. The first time was in Hamburg, where we had to find a hostel for the night before continuing on to Scandinavia. The train had arrived late at night. Confused by the phone system and with no one to direct us to the hostel, we gathered together, deciding we might need to stay in the train station. Just as we turned from the pay phone, a young man approached and asked if he could help. Yes, he knew the way to the youth hostel. Just follow him.

In hindsight, that might have been a dangerous decision. But he led us through the dark city streets to the hostel. We were so overjoyed to see it, and when we turned to thank our guide, there was no one there. He had slipped away into the darkness. But we also wondered how he could have disappeared within just a few seconds. I've never quite given up on the sense of an angelic presence.

Once we were in Norway, we knew we didn't want to stay in the city of Oslo and found the address for a *pensjonat* (small hotel) in the mountains in our guidebook. It was a beautiful trip by bus, and it seemed delightfully idyllic to me to have the road blocked by a herd of sheep. As we wound up the mountain, higher and higher into the alpine, the houses thinned out into a vast pine forest. At last the bus stopped at the small hotel where we wanted to stay for the night. It was only after the bus pulled away, and we had walked up to the door that we realized the pensjonat was closed. At almost the same moment, big, puffy flakes of snow began to fall around us. We looked at each other, wide-eyed. We could see no other buildings in the area. And the road was deserted. We pulled the hoods of our coats closer around us and shivered. And then—a tiny car came around the bend in the road, slowed, and then turned to stop beside us. A small woman asked us in English, "Do you need some help?" When she heard our predicament, she offered us one of her summer cottages that she rented out to tourists.

"They're not really made for winter, but maybe you would like them?" We readily agreed. "My name is Astrid," she said. "Get in. It's not far."

Getting into her English Morris car with all the backpacks was hilarious. The cottage itself was so cozy and picturesque that we brushed off any attempt by our host to apologize for it being cold. The pine walls, the thick down comforters, and little woodstove felt like heaven after the spare hostels we had stayed in. Out our window, pine forests spread for miles and a moose appeared in the clearing. Again it seemed Astrid had appeared like divine assistance.

Later when we were invited to Astrid's house for strong coffee and what she called pancakes, I explained that my sister and I had Norwegian ancestors. When I told her our grandmother's maiden name was Twait, our host jumped up and hugged me tight to her chest.

"That is my maiden name," she said. "We are related. It's not a common name."

I still marvel that of all the people in Norway, an unknown relative came to our rescue in a remote mountain village. Phil Cousineau writes in his book *The Art of Pilgrimage* that, "We must let go and trust in Kairos, the old god of synchronicity."

We ended up staying another night, as our host was insistent that we go with her up to their hunting lodge farther into the mountains. Like most Norwegian cabins, it had been in the family for generations.

As we pulled up, a group of men were skinning out a huge moose hung from a tree.

Inside the cabin we baked cookies on the top of the woodstove and drank strong coffee, told stories and gazed out over the landscape of mountaintops. And like good Norwegians, we set about helping Astrid clean the cabin for closing up. We scrubbed windows and cleaned out the woodstove, washed up dishes, and stripped beds. It was so picturesque and perfect that I, who had grown up in a culture that trusted the practical and logical, was becoming a believer in another way of trusting how life could unfold. Or as Joseph Campbell said in *Reflection of the Art of Living*, "Unless you leave room for serendipity, how can the divine enter in? The beginning of the adventure of finding yourself is to lose yourself."

We explored Norway for another week, once taking a narrow-gauge train down a steep mountain to a Flam Fjord, past small cottages with cans of fresh milk cooling in cold running streams, a hundred waterfalls, and moss-covered rocks.

Julie and I at Flam Fjord

Then we boarded an overnight train to Stockholm to experience the tradition of saunas and the famed train station breakfast smorgasbord—a lavish but inexpensive meal for backpackers—other travelers had told us about. The weather was turning cold. We jumped on a train heading south and into France and toward the intriguing Chartres Cathedral. A young guide named Malcolm Miller would open the deeper meanings of the famed stained glass windows of this structure that is simply a marvel of faith manifested.

Eventually our travel wound us into the beautiful Loire River valley, where the hills seemed to lie as if charmed by life, the green was soft and alluring, and a gentleness enticed us to stop and stay at the local youth hostel. The next day we toured a picturesque castle at d'Azay-le-Rideau, and I saw my first real moat. My overriding memory, however, was of shivering throughout the whole tour. We toured more local chateaus and shopped in the village that day. We laughed at the sight of an old man riding his rusty bicycle, reaching back with a long baguette to beat off a barking dog.

At the end of a long day, we found the local bus station and figured out the schedule to return to our hostel. The bus was packed when we got on, so Julie and Karen were sitting in other seats, and I felt very solitary. Not alone. I was feeling like my real self. I was awakening to a sense of who I was and to my capacities. As the bus bumped along back toward the hostel, I felt my substance. Not an idea of who I was, but a direct experience of my being. I thought, *I am this. I can travel in a foreign country, feel the glorious addiction of seeing something amazing every day, and all I need I can carry on my back. It's all right here. It's nowhere else.* Not consciously knowing it at the time, I was beginning to know myself in these new ways—sensing my body, trusting my way of knowing, letting things unfold rather than trying to make them happen.

The next phase of our journey included skiing with some Canadians who picked us up in their rented VW van in Grenoble, being enchanted by a hostel in the mountains in Grindelwald, Switzerland, and touring

Munich with easy-going Australians. And yes, drinking beer and eating pretzels, hot chestnuts, and lots of schnitzel, watching the cuckoo clock towers, visiting more churches and always more museums.

While in Munich, we saw another side of being an American. Two very old women tottered up to us and through hand gestures and a lot of head-bobbing, we confirmed we were American. They were so happy to know this, bowed to us, took our hands and shook them, then stroked them, all the while getting the point across that they were so grateful for the Americans who liberated their country in World War II. I assumed that they were Jewish—but perhaps they were Germans who simply never went along with the Nazi regime. We received their thanks graciously, although we felt undeserved of it; we had done nothing to free them. Yet they helped us remember the positive side of being an American and what our troops had done for so many. And how unlike it was compared to the discontent with the current Vietnam War.

We were midway through our trip when my sister Karen needed to return to Iowa to begin her new job. We waved to each other with white handkerchiefs as the train took off, as was the custom we'd seen at European train stations.

Julie and I would now travel on farther south. We had six weeks until December 22nd, when we had tickets to fly out of Amsterdam.

By mid-November, it was getting chillier in Salzburg, Austria. Italy was just across the border and not only was it said to be warmer, it was also so much cheaper to travel there. By this time, the pages in our traveler's check book were getting thin despite sticking to ten dollars per day in expenses—even rationing the amount of days we could have an ice cream cone. It was time for our month in Italy.

Even now I remember that month as one of the most magical times of my life. To put it simply, I relaxed. Already I had few fears about traveling and finding my way. Already life had become a day at a time. But when we crossed the border and entered this boot-shaped country, I sensed a deeper letting go. I cannot put my finger on it now, but leaving

Karen and Julie on a hill in Bergen, Norway

the industriously busy Germany and entering Italy felt like the days lengthened, the air softened, and the light itself became a more golden hue. It couldn't have been true, but that was what my soul enjoyed. A deep sigh.

In preparation for the trip, Julie and I had read *The Agony and Ecstasy* by Irving Stone about the life of Michelangelo Buonarroti. We decided to orient our trip in Italy around finding his paintings and sculptures described in the book. With a short stop in Bologna, this itinerary naturally centered on Florence and Rome. We spent two weeks in each city.

In Florence, or in Italian, Firenze, I learned that not all places in the world believed that working hard was the most important thing in life. Hard work didn't define the person; it didn't equal a person's value. In all our long talks with locals at restaurants and pubs or walking in the park, I heard something different. There was value in rest and relaxation. I couldn't quite believe that shops closed from noon to four o'clock each day so everyone could go home to rest, or as some inferred with a wink, to see the wife. The pace was different here. There was lingering over coffee and long conversations, and meals could go on for hours. I felt the tightly wound clock in me, one that held onto being on time, doing things efficiently, multitasking, working late, pushing to get done. This was how I knew myself. This was the way to be successful and find approval and make a living. Yet here was another way I hadn't imagined. It was so strange, but it intrigued me. This was also possible.

Even more deeply, I was drawn in Italy to see life through another perspective—the eye of beauty. We were having lunch with some new Italian friends who were excited to tell us about their city.

"Have you seen the *David*," one asked.

"No, but we will tomorrow," we replied.

There was a pause and incredulous look. "Not seen the *David* yet," he said. "Oh then you have not been to Firenze. The *David*, he is alive! You can look at him from one side and believe you see him. But then you look again, and he sees you. You look from another side, and he is different again. And yet his eyes will follow you, will draw you in, will ask you why, will hold all sorrow, all joy. He wants to speak to you, and you will want to answer. It is magnifico."

I remember thinking that not only he but everyone at the table spoke of this marble statue as a living person, not a sculpture that was five hundred years old. It only heightened our anticipation of seeing one of Michelangelo's most famous sculptures.

We went the very next day to the Accademia Gallery. But before we even reached the door, I had a profound moment. A small slit in the shade into the museum radiated a white light. Stopping, I saw the white light was emanating from my first glimpse of *David*. It captured me from the corner of my eye, just a moment's glance—and yet it stopped me in my tracks. I was completely taken by this striking figure in Carrara marble that exuded light. They were right. He was alive. I hurried to see him more fully once inside the museum. As instructed by our new Italian friends, I spent a long time gazing at him from all sides. It was as if he knew all the stories of all time, and all the ways one could fail, falter, and yet rise again, could love and trust God and then fall back, depending only on one's own reason and strength. The *David* could look at each of us and commiserate with our human condition—and yet in all of it, so much beauty.

There were four other statues by Michelangelo in the Accademia; four figures writhing as if trying to free themselves from blocks of rough-cut stone yet still bound. They were called "the Slaves" by some or "the Prisoners" by others. These rough and incomplete sculptures came from large cubes of marble maybe four by four feet. Unlike the mesmerizing influence of the perfect and polished *David*, they were still compelling. I could almost feel their pain, their desperate need to break free.

While the *David* mesmerized me, it was those four prisoners that drew my heart. I hadn't named it at my young age, but I knew their struggle to break free. I resonated with that fierce yearning to leave all that cultural conditioning and old beliefs and familiar ways behind to know myself as myself. We would return to see these sculptures twice more in the two weeks we were there.

It wasn't all museums and cathedrals in Florence. We frequented a local trattoria almost every night and became friends with an American guy who lived there and three of his Italian friends. We were wined and dined, taken out to dance and sing, and even taught the correct way to make spaghetti. And yes, I won't forget a kiss on an old Roman bridge under the light of a full moon.

We reluctantly left Florence with just two weeks left before our return to the States. But we needed to go to Rome, Roma, to see the last of Michelangelo's sculptures.

Rome was full of history and stories, too, but it never felt as personal or inviting as Florence. The streets were dirtier, the men more aggressive, the plazas more crowded. Yet it was still more relaxed than life as I knew it. We spent many evenings at an open bar at the plaza watching women stroll arm in arm as the men watched and drank that anise-flavored Greek aperitif called ouzo. We threw the obligatory coins in the Trevi Fountain and made the trek to the Coliseum, having lunch on those ancient stones, remembering the stories of the colossal pageantry and brutality of the gladiators who battled here for their lives. When we visited, it was quiet with only the movement and meowing of all the feral cats that called it home.

We made our way to the Vatican and were approached by a small English woman who offered to guide us to the wonders of the Sistine Chapel, where we craned our necks till they hurt to take in even a tenth of what Michelangelo brought to life on the ceiling.

We followed our list of Michelangelo's works in this city to the very last one, *La Pietá* at St. Peter's Basilica. It was the perfect ending to our quest. Unlike *David*, which filled me with inspiration and movement, the sculpture of Mary holding her dead son was quiet and still. I wondered how Michelangelo could have carved so much love, tenderness, and grief into that one piece of marble, the strokes so careful that her robe looked like muslin, and Christ's muscular arms still holding blood. In a way, I felt it was out of place. As tourists hurried by in the noisy sanctuary, I felt the sculpture was too intimate to be there near the entrance on the right. It needed a curtain and some bowing to enter.

An enduring gift of Italy was the lightheartedness of the people. No stern and stoic Germans these. It took me a while to relax with it, but soon I was giggling when the four grocers at a shop we went to in Rome every day danced us out of the shop and into the street.

An open bench—always a welcome place to rest

Or shrieking when a guy took us out for a ridiculously fast car ride down a narrow street with blind corners. Or when boys would bring us flowers and sing us songs. Or how the woman in the market loved to haggle but always with a smile, enjoying the banter. People moved more slowly, ate lunches under olive trees, drank wine and more wine. Pizza and osso bucco, spaghetti ala carbonara and Bolognese, thick crusty bread, ravioli and lasagna. Pizza handed out a half door in the middle of the afternoon. Parmigiano-Reggiano and Pecorino cheeses.

There was such happiness to cook for us and to feed us and to encourage us to eat more. So many courses. So much abundance, laughing, and generosity.

I did eventually tire of constantly interpreting poor English and trying to speak poor Italian, of hand gestures and pointing. I grew weary of the constant melodramatic advances of young men and yes, even pasta.

I would have traveled on if I had more money. I knew that I could do it and I knew better who I was. But we were down to the last page of our traveler's checks. We had done it. Three months in Europe on ten dollars a day.

We caught a cheap flight from Rome to Amsterdam and then back to Montreal. Landing in a severe winter storm on December 22nd, no flights were leaving for the next few days from that airport. We were anxious to be home for Christmas. Now being creative travelers, we got to the bus station, used the very last of our money to take a bus to Albany, New York, and bought the last two seats on an American Airlines flight to Des Moines with the credit card Julie's dad had given her for emergencies. By this time, it didn't seem like a miracle; it seemed how life unfolded for us.

It was good to be back in the States and in Iowa; I did miss my parents and siblings and old friends and, strangely, having ice in water glasses. But I would never truly go home to the place where I was born. Within minutes of walking in the door back at the farm where I grew up, my roommate from physical therapy school called from Fairbanks, Alaska. I hadn't even taken my backpack off when Mom handed me the phone and said, "It's for you." Even now the timing of it seems unreal. She offered me a job at the clinic where she worked. The Alaska pipeline construction was in full swing, and the clinic had the outpatient contract to supply health care to hundreds of workers.

"They'll pay your way up and back if you stay a year," she said. The salary was twice what I would have made in the Midwest. "It's amazing here; you can't believe how beautiful it is—and you can live with me," she added.

I wasn't done traveling. I wanted more. This unnamed pilgrimage hadn't eased the longing to know myself and the world; it had only fueled it. Still feeling the backpack on my back, knowing myself now as one who trusts synchronicity, I knew the wayless way would open right before me. This must be it. I had thought Sharon's desire to go to Alaska strange three months prior, and I was so sure I would never see her again when we parted. But now it seemed providential.

My pilgrimage would continue to the North, to the Last Frontier. Even the name spoke of adventure. I didn't even think about my decision. I said yes immediately, not knowing that it wouldn't be just another year of adventure. Alaska would become home and where I would meet the man willing to walk the Camino with me.

The impeded stream is the one that sings.

WENDELL BERRY

Chapter 5

The Rain in Spain
Falls Mainly on Us

Day 4. Pamplona to Obanos: 24.1 km; adjusted for climb: 25.8 km (16.1 miles)

Although normally dry in the summer, the month of May in northern Spain has twelve days of rain on average. So we prepared accordingly; Steve settled for a poncho and felt that was enough. I took my whole rain suit, pants and jacket with hood that had been foolproof in my backpacking ventures.

The morning of April 28 dawned clear and beautiful as we walked out of Pamplona and on to our next town. Within a few hours, we had stopped to put on our raingear while other pilgrims pulled out umbrellas. I was envying their choice as the rain suit was hot, but when the first gusts of wind swirled around us, and I saw umbrellas blown inside out, I changed my mind.

We walked steadily uphill that day toward a long ridge of wind turbines that turned with elegance and power. They seemed like a line of giant white crosses to me, and I loved their silent beauty. We were passing through fields of peas, and the aroma of the blossoms made me smile. Leap-frogging along the trail with us was a couple from Japan carrying huge backpacks. They had strapped on all sorts of cooking utensils and were wearing interesting wide-brimmed hats that looked like what I had seen rice field workers wearing, only more colorful. They spoke no English, and we spoke no Japanese, so we encouraged each other with smiles and nodding and bowing. The rain worsened, and the trail up the hill grew greasy with red mud. It stuck like glue to our shoes, forming red clay pancakes on the soles. We had to stop frequently to stomp them off. This hill is called the Alto del Perdon, the hill of pardon. Perhaps we were to remember how our misdeeds stick to us like mud!

Here, also, is the site of an old drinking fountain, called Gamellacos, a modern monument to the ancient legend of the Fountain of Renouncement, Fuente Reniega. Our faithful guidebook, *A Pilgrim's Guide to the Camino*, relates the following story: "A medieval pilgrim reached this spot dying of thirst. Disguised as a pilgrim, the devil offered to show him a spring with water if he would only renounce God. The dying pilgrim refused, and St. James himself miraculously appeared revealing the water source and quenching his thirst with water in a scallop shell."

As we neared the top, the rain stopped and we happily shed our raingear. We began to hear the soft swoosh of the turbines and see the force of their long graceful blades turning in the wind. Cresting the hill, thin metal sculptures of medieval pilgrims, rusted in the weather, were planted on the ridge. Their forms placed as if pushing on to the west, heads bent, staffs poised, leading a donkey, the mascot of the pilgrimage. We took turns posing as members of those metal pilgrims and taking pictures, needing an excuse to linger there and to play a little in all the mud. It was encouraging to see this artistic offering so far from anywhere. It was another reminder that we never walked the Camino alone; there were the spirits of so many who had gone before.

We still hadn't taken our short day, which we had promised ourselves. So we planned to stop in Uterga. Within site of the village, the skies opened, and before we had time to fully suit up, we were drenched. Oh well, the albergue was just minutes away. Or so I thought. When we walked up to the counter of the bar, the barmaid ignored us repeatedly. I know we looked like drowned rats, but we just wanted a room.

Joining pilgrims of ages past

Finally we understood that once again all the rooms were full. We sat outside on the chairs under an awning and regrouped. The next town of Obanos was 5 kilometers or so. On we would go, wet and dripping.

Here I would first notice there were really two parts of me on this pilgrimage; one was having the experience, and the other was observing it. This fascinated me. Part of me was feeling sorry for myself. Another part of me was aware I was feeling sorry for myself. One part of me was wondering if we'd ever get to the next town, and the other was assuring me that of course we would get to the next town. One part of me noticed only how cold and tired I was; another part told me to look up and see the beauty of the storm, see the tumult in the twisting clouds. These two parts would have regular dialogues on the rest of the journey.

As we now clomped in more sticky mud and flooding ditches through the spring fields, we read in our guidebook that we could take a bypass of 2 kilometers to see the Knights Templar church in the small town of Eunate. The long history of the Knights Templar would follow us in the days ahead; they were a large organization of devout Christians whose main mission was to protect the pilgrims, while also carrying out military operations. Although we had no need of these protectors now, pilgrims were preyed upon in the Middle Ages.

We came to the fork in the road and hesitated. I had wanted to walk less today, not more. My feet were aching, and one hip was complaining. But fortunately I told myself, *You'll never be here again. And you are just tired, not dying. Don't miss this.*

A wide loop spread out into flat fields in front of us. It seemed that we should be able to see the cathedral from here, but there was nothing. A stone sign sunk into the ground at ankle level simply said, "Eunate" in hand lettering with an arrow pointing the way. I needed that small encouragement to keep going.

At a slight bend in the road, the cathedral seemed to come up out of nowhere; its stately octagonal shape was alluring and beautiful. The cathedral was ringed by a running set of arches that led to the small main entrance.

It was more of a tiny chapel than a church; the flowers were fresh, and real candles were burning in front of the statue of Mary off to the side. Many of the old wooden pews were filled with pilgrims. Tired and discouraged again, I sank down to contemplate me.

A young woman in the pew in front of me was crying; she was held and soothed by her woman friend. As she sobbed, she moved me out of my self-reverie. Others were suffering on this pilgrimage. Others, too, were facing things that moved them to tears. Then I felt my body relax and accept, and I settled into meditation and prayer. I felt the strength of the Knights Templar and the unending compassion of Mary in that room. A deep peace settled on me like a grace, and I could breathe deeply and calmly, trusting that soon I would have a bed and rest. But for now the blessing of this church wanted to soak me in love and mercy. Without knowing much at the time about the Knights Templar, I could strangely still feel their presence of support and protection in this small chapel.

When we got to Obanos, the shoe rack outside the door was stacked with rows of muddy hiking boots and tennis shoes. There were many who had arrived before us. We fully expected to be turned away again, but then Juan appeared, almost bowing to us in welcome. This *hospitalero* apologized that the beds in the main dorm were taken, but he had beds in a small room that he reserved for snorers. If we didn't mind sleeping with a snorer, we could stay there. Was he kidding? No other hospitalero had seemed to care about snoring in the albergue, and I had resigned myself to many sleep-interrupted nights. These snorers defied the best of earplugs. Another cross to bear on the pilgrimage, I counseled myself. But ironically enough, that night in the snorers' room was one of the quietest thus far.

Our first Knights Templar church

The next morning we got up, packed our bags, and then tied on our boots. We had a ritual of walking about a hundred yards or so and then checking in.

"What hurts?" Steve would ask me and then I'd ask him.

We'd take an inventory of our bodies, rate the pain, and decide if it was serious. Most times we would be amazed at how well we felt after being sure the previous day would most certainly be our last, or at least we'd have to take a day of rest to recover. The pains would shift daily so that we would almost laugh during the "daily report."

Confessions: One side of my mind knew I should be grateful, and I was. But there was also a lot of faking my seeming tolerance and patience of things not going exactly as I planned. I was intermittently struggling with the "optimism and happiness" part of the pilgrim mandate. Why all this rain and no reliable place to sleep?

Day 5. Obanos to Lorca: 15.7 km; adjusted for climb: 16.9 km (10.5 miles)

We had a beautiful walk through Puente La Reina, meaning the Queen's Bridge, named after its benefactor, Dona Mayor. She had commanded the Romanesque bridge to be built over the wide Rio Arga to support the increasing number of pilgrims in the Middle Ages. Red poppies were bursting out along the roadside. We stopped at the cathedral for morning worship as it was now Sunday. It was Steve's first time inside one of these old cathedrals, and he was stunned at the size and magnificence of the altarpiece, the sound of choirs singing in those vaulted ceilings, and the ornate carvings. Although I had seen it in previous travels, I sat in awe as well. I gave thanks for the peace of Eunate; the kindness of Juan, the hospitalero in Obanos; and the beauty of the morning. "Let me trust more," I thought.

We slogged into the red mud fields again, slipping up to our ankles. We skirted the worst of it by walking through a vineyard to get on higher ground.

Climbing steeply up the streets of the village of Cirnaqui, we found a little store open on Sunday. Fresh baguettes, yogurt, and cheese raised our spirits as we lunched in the sun. Sitting and resting, I realized how different the rules of society are in Spain. Two cars met in the street in front of us. Two men talked excitedly to one another through the windows. Then the one got out, dropped his pants to show his friend a bruise on his rear end and promptly pulled them up and off they went!

We walked on to another small village called Lorca where it started raining again. Maybe we were still gun-shy of the weather, but we decided to stop after going less than ten miles that day. This would be our promised short day. We waded through a baptismal party in the café of the albergue and found the owner. It was her granddaughter who was the center of attention, but yes, there were beds available. It was a wonderful place to rest and had an area where we could wash out our clothes and hang them on the line. The sun came out again and we just enjoyed being warm and dry. I watched the baby being dressed in an elaborately long baptismal gown and joined the other women in exclaiming over the little one. Some things don't need translation. Small yet great comforts.

Confessions: I didn't like to admit that I wanted to stop after ten miles. Or that my body needed a rest day. I began to see that which I didn't want to see—my pride, plain and simple. Pride in wanting my body to defy the aging process. Pride in saying that I could walk five hundred miles and say it casually, sometimes coyly, as if we were above the challenges of the trail. Alaskans often have that kind of arrogance—at least this Alaskan did. I think back now to the shadows I saw at the beginning of the trip; the shadow of the cross, the shadows of the arches. This was another aspect of the Camino: it would be a journey of seeing my own shadow. Shadows like my pride, the narcissistic need to be perfect, my unrecognized prejudices, and my lack of trust. Unlike other shadows, these shadows I would step on again and again.

Day 6. Lorca to Los Arcos: 30 km; adjusted for climb: 31.8 km (19.8 miles)

At midmorning Steve sampled the red wine that flows out of a spigot at an old monastery in Irache; it's free for pilgrims. Fortified, we climbed past the beautiful fields of red poppies, through winding trails of forests, and up a steep incline to a mountain village. It was about noon and we could have stopped there, but it seemed early, so we pressed on. As we were coming down the mountain through the vineyards, it was impossible not to notice a huge black rain cloud looming on the horizon and bearing down on us. We could see the next village and thought we could make it, but we donned our raingear just in case. In Alaska, most of the time the rain is more of a heavy mist with occasional downpours. We aren't strangers to a wet climate, but we were not prepared for the deluge

Steve drenched in the storm of the century

of cold, stinging rain propelled by 40 mph winds. Dismayed but awed by the downpour, we ran into the next cluster of buildings. It felt like someone was pouring a bucket of water over us.

Villages close down from one to four o'clock for the afternoon meal and siesta as I had experienced in Italy. Mostly I think this is a lovely idea. Such a different way to organize life and to honor the need for the body to rest and enjoy food. But sometimes, my American side wanted shops to be open when I wanted them open, and this was one of those times. We searched and searched for a place out of the rain, finally finding an open café, but not before we were drenched on the inside as well. Steve's poncho had whipped so much in the wind that the water had seeped in, and I had sweated heavily from running. The Gore-Tex hadn't "breathed" as promised. We stripped off our wet outer clothes and sat down at an open table, steaming. *Whew. Okay. It's pouring, but we're okay and it's time to eat. We'll have a nice leisurely midday meal,* I thought.

Having studied Spanish prior to the pilgrimage, I had mastered the basic phrases for getting around. Unfortunately, I had learned just enough to form the sentences and speak them with a fairly good accent. Unfortunately, because it was good enough for the Spanish to think I would understand their rapid reply, full of idioms and their own local accent. So when we ordered, we rarely knew exactly what we would be getting. At this restaurant, we decided the best thing was to go with the plato de dia—the plate of the day. Really it's more than one plate. There's always plate one and plate two, and then dessert. Hot steaming ham and potato stew was our first plate. It restored our wet and sagging spirits with its hearty nourishment. That would have been enough for me; but it was followed by a pork cutlet and fried potatoes. Then dessert, cake and coffee. As we finished lunch, a bus came by and a flock of other pilgrims stormed the bus to get a ride to the next town. Of course—we did not. There was a break in the rain, and optimistically, we set out again on an adventure that, in hindsight, I'm glad I didn't miss.

The culverts were flooded with red water, the color of the soil in this area. We had to jump and climb around the surging, foamy water and slog through mud and mud puddles. My socks were soggy and my boots made a steady squishing sound. The sun came out, and we were seduced into taking off our raingear and trying to get dry again.

We walked past sloping fields planted in white asparagus, long rows of mounded dirt, covered in black plastic to keep the asparagus from forming chlorophyll. White asparagus is a mainstay in this part of Spain. Every ensalada mixta (mixed salad) had one or two big spears of it on top. And since it is the only choice for salad, I had it quite often. I once tried to order a Caesar salad for variety when in a larger city, but it was really an ensalada mixta with croutons.

We continued through a hilly, rural area where the fields changed to the green of wheat and barley. I hadn't expected to see this many cereal crops in the area, but there were acres and acres of spring green stalks swaying in the wind like sweeping waves, changing from green to silver as the wind brushed a huge hand across the surface. And then it began to rain again.

There was no one else on the road that we could see as another huge storm system blew in behind us. As the rain came down harder and harder, I pulled my hood up tighter around my face, blocking my peripheral vision, and leaned over to steady myself in the wind. It was becoming a bit demoralizing after another hour or so of trudging along, and it was hard to talk as the storm blew harder so I switched on my iPod to listen to some Celtic music. Perhaps it would buoy my spirit. I was soon lost in reverie.

At that moment, lightning flashed, and the skies overhead thundered at exactly the same time. I was jolted back to the road and the storm. It was right overhead! Maybe we should find shelter. Then I noticed that it wasn't we anymore; Steve was nowhere in sight. *Must be hunkered down in the ditch,* I thought. But I saw nothing when I looked ahead and behind me repeatedly. The lightning cracked again. Maybe he was in that small stone shed in the corner of the field. I ran ahead to look in. No Steve. I began to get worried. Had he been struck by lightning? There was a bend in the road up ahead, so I convinced myself he had just gotten ahead of me and was out of sight. But something didn't feel right. Maybe I shouldn't be standing up in this field with lightning striking the ground? I hurried up the road, a little desperate to catch sight of him. But when I turned the corner, my heart sank. I could see the road winding ahead a mile or so, but there was no sign of Steve. Maybe he had been struck by lightning and fallen in the tall grass. Believe it or not, the song playing on the iPod was "Calling on Angels" and the lyrics, "Help me through this one, don't leave me alone." Where was he? Where was I? I not only felt lost on the trail, I felt lost inside.

The word *lost* comes from the Old English word los meaning "to come to destruction, to perish." It was at that moment on the Camino when there were no scallop shells, no yellow arrows, and no companion that I truly felt the Old English meaning of the word. I was feeling dismantled and even questioning whether I would perish in that storm. In that moment I didn't know where I was or who I was—exactly the work of the Camino. It's painful work to destroy the ego. To see how fragile that ego is and how it is based so fundamentally on fear and the need to know and be in control. As I stood on that turn in the road, it was the turning that I needed. To not know. And in that, to take another step on that spiral staircase of coming to my true self.

In *A Field Guide for Getting Lost*, Rebecca Solnit writes, "Leave the door open for the unknown, the door into the dark. That's where the most important things come from, where you yourself came from, and where you will go." Just for an instant, I knew myself stripped of all the ways I mask up. It was clear and, in a word, terrifying. I wasn't able to stay in that place of not knowing while the rain was pouring down and the lightning flashing. The feeling of utter aloneness was overwhelming. Yet it was showing me the way, yielding up a secret of coming to the realization I sought; like the lightning, it was a flash of where I would go on my spiritual path in the years to come.

I turned to retrace the road, my stomach in a tight ball of anxiety. Then way off to the right, a piece of moving red caught my eye. I looked closer. It was a person. And then another person. It must be pilgrims. But what were they doing way over there? Then it struck me. What was I doing way over here? With my head down, looking at my feet through the tunnel of my hood, I must have missed a turn! I scanned backward from the pilgrims I'd spotted, and there, waving his arms over his head, I finally saw Steve. His green poncho blended perfectly with the wheat fields. No wonder I hadn't seen him. Relief flooded me. He was okay. Almost immediately after that huge sigh of relief, chagrin; I'd walked a mile out of my way on an already long and tiring day. And I was still shaky after that moment of feeling so vulnerable and alone.

As I jogged back and found the small yellow arrow that pointed left on the stone monument, I saw how easily I missed the marker on the road.

I could see Steve was watching my face as I approached, wondering if I was really frustrated or mad.

"I thought you got struck by lightning," he said.

"I thought you got struck by lightning," I countered. Then we both burst out laughing, as we recounted to each other what had happened.

We walked, grateful for being together. The rain let up, but we still had a couple hours of walking to Los Arca, our next destination. I got so tired, I felt a strange giddiness. I finally sat down by the side of the road and let the Camino do its work of reorienting my soul. That surrender. I do remember watching sheep on a hillside strangely enough. I saw a lot of commotion in the herd and strained to see what was chasing them. Then I realized it was a very well-trained sheepdog being guided by the owner near the barn, using simple hand gestures. It was fascinating to watch the dog cut one sheep out of the herd and guide it to the barn where they were shearing. I sighed, wishing my guidance was as obvious and that I was that well-trained.

But there was nothing to do but get up and keep walking in my squishy boots. At last the town appeared; it felt like salvation. Steve and I trudged up to the first albergue.

"I'm sorry, we've been full since two o'clock," the host said. "You might as well catch a bus to the next town as the whole town is full."

"You mean all the albergues?" I said, as I knew there was another one.

"All the hostels and hotels as well," she said. "It's May Day tomorrow, and Spain takes a holiday. There's a lot of Spaniards taking a long weekend and walking the Camino for a few days. So the place is booked. The next bus is at the square at six thirty."

She was so matter of fact, and I was so tired. *A holiday?*

"Wait," I wanted to say. "I've walked eighteen miles. And I'm wet, and albergues are supposed to help pilgrims find a place to stay." But I didn't. In my disgruntled state, I imagined all the other pilgrims, some who had taken the bus, were looking at me smugly.

We went to the square in front of the cathedral where the bus would come through, but we were still so set on walking every foot of the Camino that the thought of catching a bus was insulting. We also had quickly discovered that you could never really trust hearsay about the beds available. So we went to the other albergue; often if you stated your plight, the mayor would open up a gym somewhere. But this host was like the gestapo of the Camino.

"On the floor?" he asked, as if I'd suggested the impossible. "There's a fire code after all. Can't do it. Sorry. Take the bus to the next town."

We began asking other pilgrims where they were staying, and soon a very helpful group of Spaniards tried to help, using their cell phones to call places. Just then a man came up and said, "It's only a garage floor, but I think I can get you into this place. The woman doesn't want to let anyone use it, but I've made her feel guilty, so she let in some other women. Maybe she'll let you stay as well."

At this point, I was beginning to see a reenactment of the Christmas story. Two tired travelers come to town. (Although neither one is pregnant.) No room at the inn. Offered a place to sleep not usually used for accommodation. This man was playing the role of innkeeper. He did convince the woman to let us stay in the garage. We even knew our roommates—a group of South African women who were in their late sixties, full of fun and determination despite the fact they were fairly out of shape.

The garage was piled with stuff like most garages, but the good part was that it was at least tiled. We weren't on a dirt floor. However, that made it cold and hard. The helpful man, feeling sorry for us, borrowed blankets from the albergue of the gestapo.

"Don't tell him I gave them to you," he said. Now I surmised he was like one of the three wise men bearing gifts. Those blankets saved the day, as the temperatures fell to forty degrees that night. We ate day-old baguettes with some old cheese and some squares of chocolate; we were too tired to go looking for food. As we made our little nest on the floor, we realized we were sleeping in the path of everyone who was traversing to their cottages in back of the garage. They were sympathetic to our arrangement as they passed by on their way to warm comfortable beds, but it made me feel pathetic.

Our South African friends coped with the situation by getting a big bottle of whiskey. Soon they were singing Beatles songs and had a contest of trying to stand on their heads. They made us laugh, and then I could hear myself thinking, *You'll make it through the night, and you'll remember this night more than any other on the Camino.*

Outwardly, I didn't whine, but this wasn't what I'd expected on the pilgrimage. It wasn't supposed to get this cold. My hips were so sore that I couldn't lie flat and had to prop them up on the seat of an old folding chair. I put my damp clothes inside my sleeping bag with me, knowing they'd never dry overnight on the line. As I laid down at last, the May Day bands and revelers were hooting and hollering. Firecrackers were going off, and dogs were barking in symphony.

This too shall pass, I thought, then after a few more minutes of noise I thought less philosophically, *Shut up.*

Confessions: I was trying to do it perfectly. Steve and I had made the decision that we would walk the entire pilgrimage. We had already heard about other pilgrims who had decided that the middle part of the Camino, called the meseta, was just a flat, boring plain, too windy or hot to enjoy. So they would take the bus from Burgos to Leon, two large cities on either end. But not us. We would keep on the Way. We had also decided that we, toughened and trail-wise Alaskans, would not jump the bus or take a taxi if it rained or if we were tired, as we saw others do. We would always walk. And not only would we always walk, but we would always take the original trail rather than the road that sometimes paralleled it and was easier walking. Oh dear, it's hard to look back at all that self-righteousness. And how we got our comeuppance.

Day 7. Los Arcos to Viana: 19 km (11.8 miles)

In the morning, we woke up around six, stiff and needing to use the bathroom. Steve had only brought a silk sleep sack and even in all his clothes, he had a cold night. A man was sleeping perpendicular to me, one of a couple from Canada who had come in even later than us. He sat up with his mummy bag drawn up tight around his face, looking exhausted.

"I guess nobody said it would be a rose garden," he said, philosophically.

Today would be better, we thought. But it rained steadily as we began walking at the crack of dawn. Soon the wind began blowing, and the rain came at us nearly horizontally. The original trail on this section of the road was a red dirt path that wound up and down steep gullies. We could see that many pilgrims were taking the pavement that intersected the path at various places. But we were determined to take the Camino.

By noon we were nearly hypothermic. Because of the holiday, there were no little shops open where we could stop for hot coffee or tea or be bolstered by some wonderful morning pastries. The wind had whipped Steve's poncho into branches of a tree, tearing it open in three places. He was getting soaked. He finally ducked into a small cave to try and duct tape it together again. I was afraid to stop. The temperature kept dropping, the rain nearly close to sleet, and I realized I was stumbling at times. This was the place where I fell in the ravine and my face was pinned in the rocks and mud.

Steve turned and was coming back to help. I could see he was ready to burst out laughing at the sight of my face. He later told me that my response was the best quote of the trip: "It's a good thing this was my idea to walk the Camino," I said.

You have to understand that there is history here between Steve and me and having adventures. We make regular pilgrimages to our cabin in Alaska. It's a beautiful site that sits on a lake with a clear view of Denali—the tallest mountain in North America. It's framed in the large window just opposite the big kitchen table. We watch it change in the light and weather for hours—our own version of television. There's no road to our cabin, five miles as the crow flies from the Parks Highway. Steve staked this ten acres back in the sixties in a state program called Open to Entry. You could have the land simply by paying for the survey. Whenever we go these five miles into the wilderness, we have learned the hard way never to take nature for granted.

So when I fell face first in the mud on the Camino, there were echoes of trips to the cabin that were Steve's idea. Like the time we were going in with our kids and got stuck in overflow—water that is pushed up from the lake in heavy snowfall yet is hidden under the top layer of snow. When you pull up from the water, everything that it has touched turns instantly to ice—perilous when it's ten below and the track on the snowmachine looks like a small iceberg. Or the time we came in September and kept falling up to our necks in the small but deceptively deep, narrow creeks that laced the swamp. Or the time it had rained so much that we had to build bridges by cutting spruce trees by hand to cross creeks, now raging. Most of the time Steve has been the one to lead us into these uncomfortable adventures. But this time, I had to take the credit.

We could tell as we walked into town that the weather was surprising the locals as well. People came out to meet us with umbrellas and kept murmuring what I assume was sympathy for us and shaking their heads as they gestured toward the sky. By this time I was shivering with cold and still the rain came down. We were so happy to enter the arches of

Viana, five hours after starting out that morning. We went to a pensión that the guidebook suggested, thinking we deserved a private room to recuperate after the night on the garage floor. But it was . . . *full*. As we turned to leave, wondering again where we would sleep, the woman of the house came out on the balcony and began shouting to her husband who had answered the door. He motioned for us to come into his shop that adjoined the house, and began calling on the phone while we dripped on the floor, and his wife brought us cookies.

Soon I figured out through his broken English and my broken Spanish that they had a friend who sometimes took in guests although she normally wouldn't be open this early in the season. Finally they got through and yes, she would take us in! We followed the directions down a narrow street and finally found the number on a massive wooden door that looked to be several centuries old. In fact, it was.

Juana opened the door to us; unable to speak a word of English, she was clearly horrified at our condition and anxious to show us hospitality. We ducked under the low doorframe into a huge dark entry, full of old armor, pictures of St. Mary, crucifixes, and massive black furniture with chairs of worn red velvet. Off to the side was a small chapel, a mainstay in the old Spanish house, with kneelers for prayer, white candles dripping wax, and dusty silver crosses of all sizes scattered across a tiny altar. The whole place felt old, and the floors of stone were ridiculously uneven. And yet, Juana's hospitality made it feel like refuge.

We followed her up a wide winding staircase with a skylight overhead that let us hear the still pounding rain. She led us to a room decorated in pink brocade and faded lace. A sagging brass bed was tucked into a niche and an old glass lamp hung on single cord of a broken fixture. Nothing had ever looked so good. Taking our wet clothes to dry on the balcony and giving us newspapers for our boots, Juana left us with vague directions to the shower upstairs.

We stood in the shower longer than is environmentally conscious as we tried to get our core body temperatures back to normal. Putting on our long underwear, we jumped into bed and had a picnic lunch on the silk coverlet, now able to laugh and marvel at our morning. Listening to the rain pour down outside our window, we closed our eyes and rolled together to the middle of the soft mattress. We slept for four hours. Later we would learn of the freaky May First storm that swept across Spain. Millions suffered in widespread flooding, and Madrid was nearly brought to a standstill. At the restaurant that night we sat with a table full of fellow pilgrims, and we saw scenes of flooding on the TV playing silently over the bar. By then we were all warm again and could talk about our horrible day with a sense of honor. We'd done it! Little did we realize we were in the storm of the century and that we would hear reports about it during the rest of our walk. Pilgrims who were crossing the Pyrenees that day were hit by snowstorms and biting cold. We even began to feel lucky! I was aware that the experience was changing as my perception of it changed. All the facts were the same, yet I was seeing the experience with new eyes.

I walked for that miracle of transformation, not knowing what it would be. But already at this point in the journey, I remembered that transformation does not come easily. We are often broken down before we can be reformed. Again, like trust, this evidently was a lesson that had to be experienced again and again until it was learned.

It wasn't the first time that life experiences had broken me down so something new could emerge. Painful as it was to acknowledge those lessons, I could easily remember two very different times in my life when I had to walk that hard and difficult path that undid me before revealing its gift.

The first experience was my move to Fairbanks; the second was my first year of seminary. In both cases, it was a journey of recognizing my true support isn't external; it is coming to know and trust myself and the indwelling of the Sacred.

Confessions: I am becoming more familiar with the second commandment of the Camino: *"The authentic camino is the one going on inside each one."*

LORCA (NAVARRA)

*Sometimes it takes darkness and the sweet confinement
of your aloneness to learn that anyone or anything
that does not bring you alive is too small for you.*

David Whyte

Chapter 6

Breaking Down, Rising Up

Alaska wasn't an intentional pilgrimage. Like the European backpacking trip that ended just a month before, it was fueled by the lure of adventure, but this time a settling into my first job and a career as a physical therapist. It was born of longing to stretch myself even more into the world, even as far as the Last Frontier, still unsure of my connection to the spiritual path. Now at the age of twenty-three, I had so many questions about the religion of my childhood. I didn't see a path ahead I trusted.

When I stepped out of the airplane at Fairbanks International Airport, I immediately felt like it was home, even though it was forty below in January and the ice fog was so low to the ground that I could barely see ten feet ahead as we drove out of the airport. And what I could see were these spindly, drooping pine trees that my friend assured me weren't dead. "They're called black spruce," she said.

The landscape would open up to a new world after that first night. It became my church. All the cathedrals of Europe were no match for the glories of the mountains, rivers, and valleys that made up this northern wilderness. I arrived in the midst of the construction of the Alaska pipeline; Fairbanks had grown from fifteen thousand people to sixty thousand in three months. It would be the closest I would ever be to the experience of a boomtown and the Wild West all rolled into one. I laid aside all my questions of who I was and what was sacred and simply fell into the mire of raw experience.

Even though I had just traveled in Europe for three months, I was not prepared for Fairbanks in 1975–76. It was a chaotic mix of cultures

My first night in Alaska at a celebratory dinner

that jarred me into new realities almost every day—the military atmosphere of the nearby army base, the Native cultures of Athabaskan
Indians and Inupiaq Eskimos, old homesteaders, gold miners, private
pilots, trappers, and workers on the pipeline from countries all over the
world—all had come to strike it rich in oil.

My landlady was the former madame of Fairbanks, my first Native
potlatch served up stew with fish eyeballs in it, my first job had a keg of
beer in the basement for use during work on Alaska Day and Seward's
Day, and it was just fine if you wanted to smoke marijuana. There was
the frontier understanding of live and let live. Prostitutes literally hooked
young men with the end of an umbrella to drag them into the bars on

Second Avenue. I had gangsters standing outside my treatment rooms to protect my patient from the Mafia. I had several ridiculous proposals of marriage from men who had just met me; one told me if I married him, I'd never cook another day in my life, and I could have as many children as I wanted. I turned him down. I had bullet holes in my living room window, and we were harassed with threatening phone calls from what we later discovered was a jealous girlfriend of a friend of ours. There really were ten men to every woman; Sharon and I were invited out to dinner three or four nights a week; other times we were cooking for young men, far from home who were just lonely. One was a patient of ours from Texas who was working on the pipeline to save the family grapefruit farm. He asked us shyly if we could just cook him chicken and biscuits one night. He was so homesick.

There were so many new things that happened so fast; although I was thrilled with the adventure, my inner support felt shaky. It seemed nothing here followed the rules of my midwestern upbringing. What was right? What could I trust?

Within that first year, I had fallen head over heels for a wildlife biologist who was both wild and full of life. It was he who first mentored me in how to enter the wilderness and how to walk in it, what to notice and how to react. On our first long trip, we hiked two mountains in Denali National Park to do a Dall sheep survey. Then later in the afternoon of that day we flew into the Alaska Range in a small airplane, landed on a gravel bar, and hiked for several hours up to a Dall sheep mineral lick where he needed to do a count of sheep and lamb ratios. On the way, a huge grizzly mama and her cubs broke out of the trail behind us and ran off to the left. I'll never forget her beauty and grace as the sun hit her cinnamon brown fur, undulating from the huge musculature under her skin. My new boyfriend said simply, "She's been tracking us, but just now got our scent when the wind changed." My eyes widened.

I crossed ice-cold creeks that were up to my neck on that trip, and I climbed six thousand feet in elevation in new boots. I had grown up in the flatland; my body didn't know mountains. I was so tired and maybe hypothermic that I refused to eat once we arrived at the campsite many hours later. My friend, seeing the signs, literally kept me awake and spooned soup into my mouth before he would let me sleep: it was near 2:00 a.m.—and being summer, it was still light.

I will always be grateful for what he taught me about wilderness, spotting wildlife, understanding terrain and weather, the way of rivers rising and falling, and map-reading. I walked many miles behind him through tundra, dwarf willow, and birch brush, rocky streambeds, tortuous alders, and high mountain sheep trails, following their narrow paths that scribed all the high ridges and rocky summits.

He was one of my first patients in the outpatient orthopedic clinic where I worked, and we had become friends. When I expressed an interest in the fact he ran sled dogs, he offered to take me for an exhilarating ride on the dogsled trails that snaked around the city. This wasn't unusual—being so isolated, almost everyone adopted you as a friend. Already a patient had loaned me the use of a cabin; another had taken me flying up to Circle City to the hot springs. Another had helped fix a car. It seemed like any other friendly offer. Then things shifted.

We stopped at a small museum after the dogsled ride to look at some artifacts of dog mushing, and he slipped his hand into the pocket of my jacket to hold mine. I jerked back and felt my cheeks get red. I walked away and tried to pretend it didn't happen. I had not expected this. He was married, and I had even met his beautiful wife at the clinic. When he dropped me off, he leaned over and gave me a kiss on the cheek so gentle that an electric shock ran through me. I jumped out of the truck and ran inside, knelt on the floor, and trembled. What had just happened? I refused to see him again, even though he pleaded that he and his wife had drifted apart, and they were separating. I learned later that wasn't quite true at the time, but within the month he had moved out and filed for divorce. He kept calling and stopping by; his charisma was penetrating. When the divorce went through, I relented, even though I knew it was too soon. Not long after we began dating, we were driving down the street, and I was expressing my doubt that he was ready for another relationship. He reached under the dash and threw a small box out the window. "Those are the keys to my mistress in Anchorage," he said. "It's over." I didn't know what to say. There was a mistress too?

I try to be kind to myself in remembering this: I was young enough to think that I would indeed change him into a faithful and loving husband. And for those first few months, I was living a life of adventure that seemed to finally tap into all that had been restrained by living a life in farm country. In a tent in Mount McKinley Park (as it was called then), he taught me to fully experience myself as a woman, to love my body and its sensuality.

We didn't talk of anything but our future together. We often walked some property he owned just out of town and planned where we would build our house and have children. I wrote my boyfriend back home that I had met someone else and wouldn't be coming back as I had planned. But sometime in late summer, as much as he wanted to think he could be true to me, he wasn't. He simply said, "We said we'd always be honest with each other, so I'm letting you know that I had a fling with one of the other biologists when we were out on the project. Really, everyone does it. It's not a big thing."

But that was not my understanding of what we were building. I sunk into deep depression and cried solid for three days. I wasn't even angry at him as much as hating myself for being so naive. Some basic innocence broke in me.

And yet—this is the part that broke me further—I stayed. I let him talk me into it again and again over the next two years during our on-again, off-again relationship. Even when the emotional abuse began, so subtle I didn't notice at first, I stayed. But I had a deep, sick feeling in my stomach. A sickening I would name now as betraying myself, believing his words instead of my own knowing. Maybe because he was ten years older, maybe because he was so confident, maybe because everything seemed to go right for him, I questioned and doubted my gut feeling that I needed to end it.

Then one day he took me to the airport to catch a plane. And as we stood at the gate, I looked at him and felt some steel rise up in me; I could see so clearly who I was and who he was. He leaned in to kiss me goodbye, and I knew as he did that it would be the last time. I wrote the letter; I sent a box with his things. I must have sounded strong and sure this time. He didn't try to dissuade me.

That experience that was so painful to me was the beginning of listening to my own wisdom. And seeing what true love wasn't prepared me in so many ways to recognize a good life partner when I met Steve three months later. Although I was learning it again on this pilgrimage, it was the beginning at least of not only trusting myself but trusting whatever was unfolding. I had learned that so much can and will come from hardship. Perhaps even as difficulty was happening on the Camino, some deep part of me was remembering this lesson.

Years later, going to seminary at age forty-seven also disassembled part of my carefully constructed ego. When I arrived in Berkeley, California, in the fall of 1998, I may have had some longing and questions about church, but I had a pretty healthy sense of being a mom, a wife, a leader in the church back home, a friend to many, a retreat leader, a good PT, and an Alaskan adventurer. I was well-liked and respected and expected I would do well at school since I always had.

But by the end of day one, I was feeling less than. The first thing that happened was having a twenty-three-year-old seminarian hear how old I was and visibly wince and turn away. I felt dismissed from importance. My first experience with ageism. I really did not consider myself old at that point.

Then I began to experience the loss of identity as a good friend. Everyone was new here and open to making friends, but that takes time. Going home alone to my apartment by myself every night made me face a loneliness I hadn't expected. Not having the confidante of a husband or a close friend made me realize how much I depended on their feedback, approval, or just presence for me to know who I was. And living now in the midst of a big city with small streets and close houses felt claustrophobic after living by the woods and the river where I could see wildlife and often be in silence. The constant blaring of car horns and the buzz of traffic unsettled me as well. I didn't know how to navigate the city. It felt like a different wilderness, and I couldn't find my way.

At the same time, all my religious beliefs—those long-held, those questioned, those just forming—were in a huge theological jumble as the professors encouraged us to start again, to look at everything as if it was brand-new. I loved this. It was one of the reasons for going to seminary, yet I hadn't realized those beliefs were still holding ground for me. Again, things felt shaky.

I was feeling formless in a sense one Saturday morning on a sunny fall day in 1998 at the Delaware Apartments, battling cockroaches in the kitchen (another new development) when the postman slid a huge box through my open door and said, "Delivery!" Surprised, I saw the box with my name on it in the handwriting of a good friend. When I opened it, it was full of small presents from a large group of girlfriends, all wishing me well. I immediately felt like myself again. But then I thought, *So I am only myself when others validate me?* Now in the discipline of questioning everything, I was able to see how these self-images as friend and member of a family were keeping me from knowing who *I am*. Who am I without the external supports? And so again, the Camino was stripping away these same self-images just as seminary had. Hopefully I was coming to the already-asked questions with a little more awareness and wisdom this time around. But when you are in the literal mud of disintegration, tired and weak and discouraged, it's hard to believe it's transformation.

There were a lot of masks I was still wearing when I went to seminary, but that yearning was the prowling force that led me to leave home and family to see if this might be the way. I almost dropped out of seminary with a year left, still unsure if I would fit parish life. That came to a climax when I was on retreat during training to become a spiritual director, which I was taking concurrently with my third year of seminary.

I had been walking in a side garden of an old monastery near Baltimore where the retreat was held. Most of the rooms of the monastery were now empty like monasteries and nunneries in much of the world. I came upon old weathered stone markers, some so beaten down that it was hard to read the inscriptions. Slowly it dawned on me that I was walking the stations of the cross. It's a Catholic tradition, not mine, depicting scenes leading up to Jesus's crucifixion. By then I was exploring non-orthodox thoughts of what the crucifixion meant. Did Jesus really have to die to save us from our sins? Did God really need that kind of atonement? What need was there for sacrifice? I believed the story of the crucifixion; it made total sense to me that what Jesus said and did threatened the church and political leaders so much that they had to get rid of him to retain their power. I knew a lot of enlightened people who were killed for telling the truth. Could I preach with my own truth?

As I was wandering this old stone path through the markers, it was a warm, summer day. I remember the bees buzzing on tall wildflowers that had grown up between the markers. I was so torn between being pulled toward church and backing away. I stopped and, since no one was around, I said out loud, "Okay God. Do you want me to be ordained or not?" And immediately I heard this equally loud reply—"I don't care!"

It was such a surprising answer, both in that I felt I had actually heard a voice and in what the voice said. I began laughing and couldn't stop. I was making this whole path to ordination that same walk as the stations of the Cross—heavy and tormented. In truth, I felt free again with those words. And not in need of a yes or a no. I was drawn back into a relationship with the One I sought—who in that moment sounded like a frustrated parent. I was asking the wrong question.

I returned to seminary and told my advisor that I might not complete my senior year. I was contemplating a life as spiritual director and a well-educated layperson in the church. I felt my daughter needed my support in her senior year in high school, and it was getting to be too much flying back and forth. My advisor looked at me and said, "You are a great pastor already. Your internship proved it. We are going to make it work."

I was given credit for all the work I had done prior to coming to seminary and only needed to complete two more mentored classes, most of which I could do at home. I had totally surrendered to not being ordained, yet the door opened for me.

My ordination ceremony was so full of light and love that it seemed to confirm that I had chosen the right path. The church was packed, standing room only. Members of the high school class that had gone to Mexico with me on a mission trip led me into the service as they danced. Friends came from near and far. A huge choir sang. Members of my internship congregations showed up to support me. Pastors gathered wearing red, the color of the fire of the Spirit. My best friend from seminary, wearing red high heels (as I hoped she would), came from her congregation in Iowa to preach. The Hmong, who were part of the congregation and who I had come to know so well while visiting them in trailer courts all over the city, sat quietly, filling two rows of pews. And a few members of the homeless community who frequented our church were there as well. One of them regularly called out, "Praise the Lord," during the service. I loved the reality and diversity of those gathered. My mother and husband put the stole on my shoulders. But the ordination itself was what imprinted my soul.

As I knelt before the bishop to have his hands laid upon me, he called the other pastors to stand and lay their hands behind me. And then the

Newly ordained!

whole congregation stood and did the same. The blessing of over 250 people flowed into me, and their love and support and affirmation of my call nearly overwhelmed me with love. As I knelt there, I bowed my head and said to my innermost self, *I will hold the people in my heart.* It was a vow that came unexpectedly but with great clarity. This vow was what I felt I would be breaking if I left the congregation. I would not be holding them in my heart.

At that time I didn't fully understand the breadth and depth of Love. I didn't understand I would never be separate from them or any person.

And so long as you haven't experienced this:
to die and so to grow, you are only a troubled guest
on the dark earth.

GOETHE

Chapter 7

Learning to Be Helpless

Day 8. Viana to Nájera: 38 km (23.8 miles)

We blessed Viana as we left through its beautiful arches and looked out on the plain below. It was forecast to be a sunny day, and although still crisp in the early morning, we again walked with high spirits.

At this point Steve and I were both on the same physical journey but different interior wanderings. He has a more steady path and is usually unfazed by adversity. Often while I was soul-searching every event, he was paying attention to the landscape and the flora and fauna with not much worry about how his soul was doing; he is graced in that calm acceptance of many things. I think it comes from so many hours in the wilderness as a child.

Logrono was 9 kilometers away, an industrial city with wide, paved pathways for the Camino travelers. Just as we descended into the city, Steve pulled up lame, his left shin suddenly spasming with every step. Usually these things work themselves out, but Steve finally had to stop. I worked on the muscle, and we found him a staff to lean on, but our walking slowed down considerably as he hobbled along. Maybe the cold of yesterday had done more damage than we thought.

We decided to go on to Navarette, which should be easily reachable by three o'clock in the afternoon. We reasoned that since the holiday was now over, there should be plenty of rooms. The day grew hot, but the trail led around a lovely bird sanctuary where we had another picnic and rested Steve's leg. The path ran beside a less scenic part of the

Camino with a busy highway of incessant truck traffic on one side and a factory on the other. We walked beside miles of chain-link fencing that separated the two. Pilgrims have attempted to save this part of the Camino by weaving crosses into the fencing with grasses, bark, twigs, or string. It too bears testament to the thousands that have taken this path. Crosses of every size and shape decorated the fencing as far as we could see. We added two of our own as truckers honked and waved at us while passing.

Although you walk the Camino alone in many ways, you are surrounded not only by fellow pilgrims but also by the traffic passing by. At first I was startled when a truck would honk loudly. When I looked up from watching where I was putting my feet, I saw a trucker grinning widely, waving and giving me a thumbs-up or yelling "Buen Camino!" I recalled the many centuries that Spain has been welcoming pilgrims and how the tradition still lives on, even as society has become mechanized and moves more quickly. Still there is at the soul of Spain, a reverence for the holy and a history of sacred ground.

When we got to Navarette, my skin was salty with sweat. There were several albergues and hostels here so I wasn't too concerned about finding a place. But again, we were turned away once, twice, three times, four times. One of the hosts called ahead to Ventosa, a small village where there was an even smaller refugio for pilgrims. They had four beds left but couldn't promise they would be there when we arrived. But what was our choice? I was yet unwilling to sleep outside on the ground.

I began to walk ahead of Steve, anxious to get to Ventosa. It would mean we walked 30 kilometers, or 18 miles, that day again.

Finally I was too tired to hurry anymore. Steve caught up with me, and we followed this incredibly winding road to Ventosa. It was the longest 7.5 kilometers of the entire trip. But what a beautiful old town. Ancient buildings and cobblestone streets curving upward to a worn stone church. The refugio was located just below the church. I saw a young man dressed in a loose white shirt with long locks of black hair falling to his shoulders. If ever I met Jesus on this trip, it was when we met the hospitalero here.

He was guiding an older woman, who was crying, to a van, comforting her when I first saw him. Then he saw us and came to meet us. "Welcome," he said. "I see that you are tired. We have no more beds but do not worry. My friend here, the electrician, will take you to Najero in his van. All will be well. There are many places there. And you can help Nalida who is needing a room, too, and very exhausted."

In an instant we were herded into the van, hugged and kissed by the hospitalero as we settled into our seats. The electrician was a jolly sort and kept up a steady conversation with Nalida, trying to cheer her up and dry her tears.

The decision to get into the van never really felt like a decision, only like a gift. So it wasn't until we were moving down the highway did we realize that one of our resolutions for the Camino had been broken! We weren't walking these 9 kilometers—and we didn't care a bit. Now it seemed a silly, self-imposed rule. In fact, our guidebook mentioned that the pilgrims would not hesitate to get a ride in a cart if it were offered. I was immediately aware that my self-righteousness badly needed some reining in. As we rode along, Steve kept saying, "Everything is moving by so fast. Everything is moving by so fast." We had become used to a slower pace without knowing it.

Nalida was a grandmother from Brazil who had scandalized her family when she announced she was going to Spain to walk the Camino. She was in her mid-sixties but looked much younger and was stunningly beautiful. By the time we'd gone the 9 kilometers to Najero, she had pulled herself together, and with her excellent Spanish, negotiated a room for the three of us in a hostel. It cost a bit more than usual, but we were past caring at that point. Steve and I showered, washed clothes, hung socks out the window to dry, and went exploring to give Nalida a little space. She was too tired to move.

It was a funny reality of the Camino that after walking all day, most pilgrims went walking again in the evening. One always wanted to explore the town and find dinner. But this kind of walking was more leisurely and, of course, without packs.

There is a wide and clear river that runs through Najera called Rio Najerilla, and we stopped on top of the bridge for a long while just to watch the water and let the sound put us back together again. It had been a long day. We wandered streets and looked in the windows of shops. It was tempting to buy some souvenirs but easy to resist when you knew you had to carry them hundreds of miles on your back.

We had pizza that night—a sweet change from the usual fare. Even after a week, it became apparent that the pilgrim menu would be agonizingly similar. There was a special pilgrim menu provided in the towns along the Camino not only because it was cheaper for the pilgrims but because it was served at seven o'clock, two hours earlier than the usual Spanish dinner hour. Most pilgrims were too hungry and tired to wait until nine o'clock at night to eat. The menu usually cost eight euros—about twelve dollars. It included carafes of red wine or sparkling water, bread, and then your first plate was a choice of macaroni (pasta with tomato sauce), ensalada mixta (greens with tuna, corn, white asparagus, cucumber, tomato, and carrots with a vinaigrette dressing—forget choices of dressing!), soup, or a serving of vegetables. The choices for the second plate were something like beef stew, fish of some sort, a pork cutlet, or baked chicken. Dessert was rice pudding, yogurt, ice cream, and sometimes cake. After seven days of this, however wonderful and filling, a pizza was a grateful exception.

In the morning, we parted with Nilida, never to see her again on the Camino, but she wrote in our book, "Que encontro! [What an encounter!] Brasil y Alaska en Camino de Santiago! Amen."

The faces of pilgrims were beginning to imprint themselves in my mind. I wondered if the people that we met hadn't been by chance but destined to either teach us something or to see a reflection of self. As far as

Nilida was concerned, I will remember her honest tears, her shining face when she spoke of her decision to defy convention and walk the Camino alone, and her determination to keep walking. Her black eyes were flashing, her heart able to be broken and mended, but her faith steady.

I wrote in my journal that night, "The Camino is so busy; it's becoming a rush to get to a town to get a bed. Should we adapt to this? Do we become competitors then instead of supportive fellow pilgrims? Or perhaps this too is part of our journey and what we are to learn."

Confessions: I noticed something inside me I wanted to ignore. An impatience to get going—motivated by seeing how many other pilgrims were passing us by. "Remember, we are going to walk in a relaxed manner," Steve said. I nodded, but the urgent feeling that I recognized as competition wouldn't go away. When I walked, I noticed I liked catching up to slower pilgrims or computing our kilometers per hour rate of walking. Even worse, I found myself hating to stop and take a break, as all the pilgrims we just passed might catch up, and we'd have to pass them again. So much for a relaxed manner of walking. And it was humbling to realize our pride again in vowing to walk every inch of the Camino and how that goal was taken from us so smoothly.

Day 9. Nájera to Santo Domingo de la Calzada: 21 km; adjusted for climb: 22.5 km (14 miles)

An easy day—just 14 miles. I've come to learn that if my body was voting, it would like this distance. It seems anything beyond that, and I'm much more tired. The walk today was an earnest walk. Without saying anything, I think we resigned ourselves to the schedule that would better ensure a place to sleep—up early and on the trail before seven o'clock; then walk fast enough to get to the next albergue by one o'clock or at the latest, two. We walked today in open country until coming to a new development near Ciruena.

After Ciruena we began a gentle downhill walk into Santo Domingo de la Calzada and headed immediately down a narrow street to the albergue, Abadia Cisterciense, run by Cistercian nuns. At last when I offered up my pilgrim passport, it was stamped! There was room. Donations accepted.

The cloister was built in the twelfth century and probably was delightfully cool in the hot summers. But in the spring, it was cold and dark. We were assigned our beds, the top and bottom of a bunk, secured our blankets, and went down to the kitchen to eat lunch. Here we met, Iris, a Danish woman, also in her sixties and also walking the Camino alone.

"My husband would never do this," she said. "But I must call him every night so that he doesn't worry." She made us a cup of mint tea and, as many pilgrims did, asked us about living in Alaska. It was her dream to travel there in two years after retiring. She had her share of Camino adventures as well, once going nearly 4 miles in the wrong direction before realizing her mistake. That had shaken her confidence, as her husband had told her that she would never be able to find her way for five hundred miles. But she had persevered, like Nalida. Her smooth and serene face was calming, and she had studied two years of Spanish so that she could communicate better on the trip. She knew three other languages as well, having lived and traveled extensively in her life. Steve and I were frequently envious of the European's ease at switching from one language to another, while we struggled with a few basic words.

Santo Domingo de la Calzada apparently had something to do with roosters. Everywhere we looked there was a red rooster symbol on posters and in cafés, bars, and on signposts. Surprisingly there were chickens in a coop in a chapel as well. We were soon to learn this legend, one deeply ingrained in Camino lore.

The story is called alternatively the Miracle of the Cock and Hen or The Hanged Pilgrim. The legend has several variations, but the basics of it involve a pilgrim couple and their son who are on the road to Santiago. While stopped in Santo Domingo to eat, a young barmaid took a fancy to the young man and made advances. He, being a devout pilgrim, rejected her, and in revenge she planted a silver cup in his sack and reported him to the police for theft. The innocent boy was caught by police and hanged. Somehow the parents had gone ahead to Santiago oblivious of what had happened and only encountered the boy on their return, where they found him hanging but still alive, thanks to the intervention of Santo Domingo. They ran to the sheriff to beg his release and found him just sitting down to dinner. When he heard this news, he said that their son was no more alive than the cock and hen he was about to eat. On that cue, the cock and hen jumped up, and the cock began crowing. The miracle convinced the sheriff of the boy's innocence, and he was cut down and pardoned.

This was just one of many miracles ascribed to Santo Domingo, and this town became known as a place of miracles.

What does a twenty-first-century pilgrim do with these stories of miracles? Do I enjoy the story and attribute the rest to the superstitious nature of medieval Europe? Or do I allow the possibility of miracles?

On one hand, my Western mind dismisses these legends; yet there is a part of me that is willing to just hold the story in suspended belief, allowing the power of such a story to survive the centuries when others have long been forgotten. Isn't that a miracle as well? As a pastor and preacher, I've had to come to terms with the miracles of the Bible. I do not read the Bible literally but rather as a long and honest look at our relationship with God. I read it as story, allegory, wisdom literature, poetry, song lyrics, proverbs, historical narrative (in parts), and inspired writing of people of faith. Through all that comes the mystery of Living Word—a power beyond the words that are read. A Word present at creation that keeps creating us through this sacred text. In that mystery, which I don't pretend to ever understand, I accept the miracles.

There are plenty of religious scholars who propose rational theories on how the Red Sea was really the Reed Sea (it *was* a mistranslation), and this sea is shallow where strong winds do blow.

And, as another example, some scholars write that Jesus didn't really walk on water, but that perhaps there were ice chunks, dense algae, or well-placed rocks. These theories insult the mystery and try to take back control of the Bible in all its strangeness and ways that oppose popular thinking. These theories seem more ridiculous than the miracle story to me. I'm willing to let these miracles be mystery.

The Camino itself is a web of miracle stories, such as the cock and hen or the thirsty pilgrim. But the whole establishment of the Camino is built more on miracle and faith than the other two major pilgrimages of Christian faith, Jerusalem and Rome.

There is only anecdotal evidence that after Jesus's death, his disciple James went to Galicia, the present area of Spain where Santiago is located, to bring the gospel message to the people there, thus somewhere around 40 CE. The farthest point of Galicia is a point of land called Finisterre, literally meaning the "end of the earth," as was the common belief at that point in time. Here was the site of Druid initiation rites, which was fairly well known. It had already become the custom for the apostles to go to these sacred sites of other religions and tell "the better story." It was told that James wasn't well accepted, and he returned to Rome in 42 CE and was beheaded by Herod for his belief in Christ. His followers are said to have brought his body back to Galicia in the region of Padron and buried it in Libredon, the present site of Santiago de Compostela. Then the story fades for centuries but was held somewhere in collective memory. The story reemerged in 813 when a shepherd name Pelayo was drawn to a field by a bright light or star. Excavation there revealed an old tomb. The bishop of the area, Theodomirus, declared the falling of the star on this site a miracle. He then claimed the tomb as that of St. James, which was still rumored to be in this area. Thus the name of the site probably came from the word *compos* meaning "field," *stella* meaning "star," and Santiago, meaning St. James. Thus the town is called Santiago de Compostela, and the path to it, the Camino, meaning "road" or "way," de Compostela. It is also simply called the Way of St. James.

This supposed discovery of St. James's tomb in 813 coincided with the reconquest of Spain from the Islamic Moors, which began with the battle of Clavijo in 844. It was reported that St. James appeared as a knight in shining armor astride a white steed, bearing a sword and lopping off the heads of the Moorish invaders. His appearance turned the tide of that battle. The *reconquista* of Spain continued for centuries, but in a crucial battle that turned the tide toward the eventual success of the Christian forces, St. James appeared again on the white horse to slay the Moors and force the victory.

There is another miracle associated with Santiago that explains why the scallop shell has become the symbol of this journey. Legend has it that a young couple was on their way to be wed on the shores near Finisterre. In a storm the boat capsized and the groom was apparently drowned in the sea. However, just when all seemed lost, St. James appeared out of the water on a horse bearing the bridegroom and laid him on the sand. The horse was said to have scallop shells clinging to its mane and tail.

Later stories from the Camino, after the defeat of the Moors, again tell of the appearance of St. James on the Camino, but this time a more pastoral figure in the garb of a pilgrim, with staff and gourd, Bible and wide-brimmed hat. We saw a myriad of statues of St. James sculpted in this form along the route. St. James relics (pieces of his body and clothes) that are said to be retained in the cathedral of Santiago have too many miracles attributed to them to recount, but collectively his power in the minds and faith of the Spanish people led to his being named as the patron saint of all of Spain.

These miracle stories surrounding St. James and the Camino aren't biblical, of course, and to me are not to be placed in the same category as those miracles recorded in sacred text. Yet they are stories that have changed people's lives and have endured the test of time. There is a mysterious power in them that if not believed, at least must be respected and even loved for the story itself. "With God, all things are possible," says the Bible. If given the choice, I'll choose possibility over skepticism any day.

Back in Santo Domingo, the place of the miracle of the cock and hen, I was given yet another opportunity to examine my prejudices. It all began when Steve and I were standing at a table outside a small café in the late afternoon, trying the Spanish version of a hamburger, again looking for a little variety in our diet. Behind us we heard the clomp, clomp, clomp of horse hooves and turned to see what was coming.

The streets were glistening with the washing of a recent brief rain. With the sun at their backs, two burly men wearing long slickers, wide-brimmed leather hats, and cowboy boots, were strolling down the main street of town, holding the lead ropes of their large and powerful horses. A long-haired black dog followed obediently at the rear of this procession.

In the midst of this busy boulevard, people and cars came to a stop, staring. Children pointed. Old women whispered to each other behind cupped hands. And literally, the sea of people parted to let the cowboys pass. By now, I could see their rugged, handsome appearance. Women were swooning.

The two men tied their horses to a light pole outside the café where we stood, saying nothing, and strode into the café. We watched through the window as people vacated the seats at the counter and the two sat down for a beer. They were served immediately. There was a collective feeling that these two guys were at the least, mysterious, and possibly dangerous. Crowds gathered to take their pictures with the horses while the black dog patiently stood guard. When the men appeared again on the street, people backed off, and the men calmly untied the horses and led them out of town.

I assumed that these two were caballeros from a nearby ranch, and that caballeros were probably known for rowdiness and misdeeds when they came to town. I was totally wrong. We would meet these two many more times on the Camino for they were pilgrims too! They lived in the French Alps and had traveled the entire way by horseback, finding many difficulties in boarding their horses and overcoming prejudices about who they were; they turned out to be extremely kind and faith-filled men, who, like us, were just on a journey for the More in life. We lost track of them eventually, but we always hoped they made it to Santiago.

That night in the old stone cloister was one of the coldest thus far. And like most albergues located in old monasteries or cloisters, it didn't have much hot water. The showers themselves were clean and modern, but my shower was tepid, only adding to my shivering. But we had a bed and food, and I was grateful.

Confessions: I faced my prejudices again, separating myself from other pilgrims rather than seeing myself in them and they in me.

Irritated with the number of Germans, I learned that a German stand-up comedian, the equivalent of our Jay Leno, had written a book about his life-changing journey on the Camino—and now it seemed half of Germany was on the trail. That in itself wasn't the real problem. The irritation was that they were always waking up before everyone else in the dorms, rustling their packs before we were supposed to be up, and then charging down the trail hours ahead of the rest of us to get beds in the next town, all the while looking disgustingly fit and machinelike. I felt a little snarl inside me.

I was born when all I once feared, I could love.

RABIA

Chapter 8

To Love, to Serve

Day 10. Santo Domingo de la Calzada to Belorado: 24 km (15 miles)

We left Santo Domingo on our new and adapted schedule—up early and out early. Spain is divided into seventeen autonomias (similar to states), which elect representatives to the central democratic government in Madrid. We had already walked through the autonomias of Navarre after crossing the Pyrenees and Rioja when we came into Logrono. Now we would cross into the large autonomia of Castilla y Leon. These two regions were established in the eleventh century. When they were combined by Fernando III two hundred years later, it was not a happy union, and even today there are signs, spray-painted graffiti, and loose-leaf flyers still calling for their separation after eight centuries! Much of the Camino follows N-120, a busy freeway on this portion of the route, which our guidebook called "soul-less."

It took us five and a half hours to arrive in Belorado, just ahead of the rain. On the outskirts of town we found a new albergue that also arranged eco-tours—and it had open beds! I had a luxurious hot shower here (a precious simple thing) and washed all our clothes. Well, actually we washed half of our clothes. Since we never knew if they would dry overnight, we had to reserve dry ones to walk in.

This was the first day Steve carried my pack part of the way. He had always joked that he was coming along as my mule, and today he played that part. My feet and my lower back were becoming very sore after a week and a half of hiking. I continued to wonder if I would make it the entire way.

I remember Belorado as the place of storks. When the rain stopped that evening, we walked into town, a village full of small churches. The front of many of these churches had a tall edifice on them that rose above the roof of the church with two lower points and one high point, bearing a cross. On the top of each rested a huge stick nest of a stork, not a bird we see in Alaska. Steve and I were fascinated by their gawky shapes and precise way of placing their feet when they walked. There were baby storks peeking out of many of the nests. When I emailed this to a friend from an Internet café, she wrote back, saying she had read the following about the sign of storks:

Storks are said to be the most ancient and powerful symbols of new birth. It was also a bird believed to be sacred to the Roman goddess Juno—the goddess of home, children, and family fidelity. The stork has also been associated with the early lore of Christianity. One such story tells how the stork circled the cross, offering sympathy and strength to Jesus. It has always been considered good luck to see a stork or have one as a totem. They are symbols of new birth in your life. They reflect that on some level you are going to find life renewed and opportunities to awaken a new sense of joy and promise.

Whoever originally said this, the words encouraged me. Yes, that was a piece of pilgrimage—a looking for new birth, joy, and promise. I remembered then about the many dreams I had been having prior to the pilgrimage—dreams of being pregnant, having babies, looking for babies. Since there was no biological way and certainly no emotional desire to be pregnant at my age of fifty-six, I took this to be a spiritual birth about to happen. Certainly having the storks on the Camino seemed a good omen for the journey ahead.

The town of Belorado itself had a large open square with a medieval arcade on one end—a large overhang where sellers could bring their

The spires and storks of Belorado

wares for sale. In the hills above the square, you could see the ancient caves of religious hermits.

Confessions: We had given in and started getting up at 7:00 a.m. in the morning to get to our next stop, primarily to get a bed. I had totally succumbed to worrying every day about getting a place to stay.

Day 11. Belorado to San Juan de Ortega: 24.1 km; adjusted for climb: 26.6 km (16.6 miles)

Our guidebook had a great map of the elevation gains between towns, so we could always ready ourselves for the day's challenges. It would be a steady uphill climb of 500 meters (approximately 1,500 feet), with three small hills near the top. The trail would roughly follow the soul-less freeway for half of the route, and then break off into the countryside to the remote monastery of San Juan de Ortega, meaning St. John of the Nettle.

A midway point is the town of Villafranca de Montes de Oca, one of many rural villages which were settled when the French traveled the Camino on pilgrimage and then came back to make their homes along the route. Steve had to carry my pack again, but at ten pounds, he kept assuring me that even with the combined weight, the packs were less than the weight of his usual backpacking trips in Alaska.

The path climbed through oak and pine forests and broke out into long views of hillsides covered with lavender-colored bushes in full bloom. We stopped often to take pictures of the color and the clouds, although no one could tell me the name of the bush that was giving us so much pleasure. We dropped down into San Juan de Ortega by early afternoon, the day still cool, and rain clouds loomed and receded, laughing at us as we alternately raced to put on raingear and then take it off. At this point, I was wishing for a poncho—much easier to negotiate.

When the guidebook said "remote," I didn't understand that San Juan de Ortega was really not much more than the church with an adjoining albergue (formerly a huge monastery) and a small café. There were signs of the old village, but most of it was in ruin, piles of stones fallen in upon themselves. As we approached the small door marked *Sello*, meaning "stamp," I was apprehensive, wondering if we would get a bed or need to walk on. There was a very old man dressed in a worn brown sweater sitting at the small table by the Sello sign and a small metal box. I would not have noticed him in my apprehension had it not been for his expressive face—deeply lined with wrinkles and so yellow that I immediately thought he was jaundiced. And he most likely was. His eyes were merry and bright, intense and inviting. He asked if we wanted just the stamp (many pilgrims try to collect as many as possible along the way as they are so colorful and artistic) or if we were going to stay. Ah, there *was* room in this inn. Yes, I assured him, we were staying.

I went down to the café to get something to eat, but the place was packed, and by the time the bartender, also waiter, was able to get to me, it was too late. No bocadillos after three o'clock. I never could figure out the schedule for eating in Spain! So I settled for two bags of potato chips that I could buy from behind the bar and sat out in the sun on a bench, just warm enough to be comfortable if you stayed close to the wall. I knew the café wasn't open in the evening, and I began to wonder what we would eat that night. Although normally we were more prepared, we only had half of a stale baguette and some chocolate left in our packs.

As I sat in the sun, several different groups of people began showing up in cars or small vans, some of them obviously on tours, as their guides led them into the church and they followed with books in their hands. What was so special about this chapel? The monastery had been established in 1150 by San Juan, a disciple of Santo Domingo (of fame in the town we visited just two days ago). San Juan was known primarily for his devotion in serving the pilgrims on the Camino. This monastery was located in one of the wildest places on the trail and at a place where pilgrims were in danger from thieves during the Middle Ages. At one time the monastery must have been thriving, as there was room for fifty-eight beds in the upper hall.

The chapel itself had been built and dedicated to San Nicolas de Barri, who is said to have saved San Juan from drowning when on another pilgrimage to the Holy Land. I had waited to enter the chapel as it, too, was freezing inside, and I was still trying to warm up. But curiosity got the best of me, and I followed the tourists. Small but ornate, the chapel struck me with its white and soaring walls and ceilings. The guides remarked that the windows were made of translucent stone, marbled and beautiful. Around the entrance to the sanctuary of the chapel was a large lintel with ornate carvings. I could see the figure of Mary at her annunciation, a popular scene on the Camino, carved into the corner piece. I learned that one of the primary attractions of the chapel is the fact that it was built so that on the equinox, the rays of the sun fall upon the annunciation scene. Here again, this place began to take on the legend of miracles, many believing it to be a place that would restore fertility. When the barren Queen Isabella of Castile came here in 1477 and later became pregnant, she embellished the church even more lavishly as a symbol of her gratitude.

Because of the cold, the hospitaleros had closed off the back room of the lower hall and built a roaring fire in an old woodstove. Soon the pilgrims were huddled around the fire, reading, talking quietly, and writing in their journals. It almost approached cozy. A woman from Belgium was talking with a Canadian man about her journey.

"It doesn't seem right to walk so fast," she said. "I'm feeling uncomfortable about it. I'm traveling alone and met up with these Germans who told me this is how you do it. But somehow I'm feeling unhappy."

I was glad to hear that I wasn't the only one who felt this way. Others began to talk about their disappointments or trials and how they had hoped they would walk the Camino with a different spirit. I realized it was the first time that we had gathered collectively as pilgrims, as most times the lure of the towns or villages drew us off to different places. With no place to go, we had a chance to turn to each other and hear each other's stories. It was here that I heard one of the funniest stories about learning to walk the Camino.

An attractive, middle-aged woman with long blonde hair, dressed in new and expensive hiking attire, had an audience around her. They were all laughing loudly; she was obviously a good storyteller. When I joined the group, she was explaining how transformative the Camino had been to her.

"I lost my mother a few months ago," she said. "And I didn't know what to do with all this grief. I had read Shirley MacLaine's book called *The Camino* and somehow had this thought that doing that walk would give me time to think about and deal with it. So I'm an architect, and I was in Belize designing a new resort on an island there and decided I'd do it. I flew from Belize to New York, picked up some clothes and flew to Pamplona. Then I took a taxi to St. Jean Pied de Pont and flopped into bed at the albergue, thinking a good ten hours of sleep and I'll start my trip. The next morning someone is shaking me at 6:00 a.m. telling me to 'get up, get up' and I don't even know where I am or what I'm doing. 'Why?' I think. Then I find out you have to be out of the dorm in an hour. And there's these shared showers that you push for water, which gives you one minute and someone outside is yelling, 'I heard you! You've pushed three times and you only get to push twice.' At this point, I'm thinking what is this? So I pack up my rolling suitcase and put on my sandals, get my passport, and head up the Pyrenees."

She went on to tell us that she hadn't really paid attention to the details of the book, and didn't realize what the Camino was, other than a place to "get your head together." So she soon figured out that climbing the Pyrenees with a rolling suitcase didn't not work well. And her feet were soon freezing as she was caught in the May snowstorm. By the time she had walked three days on the trails, she realized how many wrong assumptions she had made.

"I brought heels, perfume, evening clothes with me. I was thinking, well, we'll take a walk and then people will go out and dress for dinner," she said. "I had no idea I would be exhausted and drop into bed every night. You gotta know that I was raised rich and spoiled. My dad was a self-made millionaire at thirty-five, and I never knew life any other way. But this walk has transformed me; I've learned you don't need a lot of things to be happy. And five-star hotels are great, but you miss meeting the real people."

In Pamplona, she shipped all her things to Santiago to pick up at the post office there. She bought boots, poles, a backpack, and hiking clothes. Then she went and bought lots of cheese and bread and started handing out sandwiches to the pilgrims for a day. "I thought I was learning that a pilgrim looks out for other pilgrims," she said. "I love this. I love this simplicity. I called my kids and told them I'm canceling our reservations at the Hilton for our fall trip to Rome and we're staying at pensións. The kids were silent and then said, 'Mmmmooooommmm, what's a pensión?' I talked with my sisters and all they said was, 'Are you meeting any men on this trip?' When I said that wasn't exactly the focus, they urged me stop this nonsense and come home. But I'm going to finish it. I'm going to do this. And I'm going to change how I live life."

That being said, a white taxi pulled up and she jumped in to ride the rest of the way to Burgos, a full day's walk away. I guess she needed a break from too much of this pilgrimage stuff. We never saw her again.

At 6:30 p.m. I went to Mass, putting on as many clothes as I could. Although I wasn't Catholic and couldn't understand many of the words being spoken, I welcomed the chance to be in sacred space and allow my soul to speak, rather than the growlings of my stomach or the aching of my feet. What Catholicism preserves for me is the Mystery, so I didn't need to understand. I was hoping in honoring the mystery of the Incarnation, God becoming Man, I could also be stunned at the mystery of my own incarnation.

In my meditation as the words of institution echoed off the marble walls, I wondered how I would remember this moment and how it would fit into the big picture of the Camino. I acknowledged to myself that I had come with expectations of the Camino, believing I would have a great life-changing experience or divine revelation. Then this thought came into my head: What if this is an affirmation or assurance, not a test or some spiritual pruning? What if it was an important time to walk and sing and pay attention and be blessed? Would that be enough? My default prayer came to me, the one I pray when I don't know what else to pray: "Holy One, help me to Show Up, Pay Attention, Speak the Truth in Love, yet remain Open and Unattached to Outcome. Amen."

I was surprised when the priest entered and stood behind the altar; it was the same old man dressed in a worn brown sweater who had stamped my pilgrim passport earlier. This must have been the well-known Father Jose Maria, who had been serving pilgrims for over thirty years. His words were like his eyes, intense and passionate, the contrast all the more compelling from the icy stone seats on which we sat. I was beside a girl from Bulgaria who was walking the Camino alone. She hadn't brought any warm clothes, as she had only known Spain to be suffocatingly hot. But that was in summer in the south of Spain. So we sat close to each other, shivering and laughing. Her eyes were the deepest blue, wide and calm. It was as if she held an ocean inside of them, and I so wanted to know her well. On the other side of me was an intense young man who was striding the Camino. We had passed each other often, and he was openly devout, often crossing himself or genuflecting at shrines or crosses along the way. Here at the church he was on the kneeler, deep in prayer. He turned to me and said in broken English, "It is cold here only in the stones; the Holy Spirit is on fire!"

At the end of the mass, we were invited to share soup in the fireside room. We would have dinner after all. Nearly sixty of us were crowded together at the table while Father Jose Maria and his housekeeper, Marcela, brought in a huge pot of garlic soup. It is a peasant soup, made with stock, lots of garlic, and then thickened with bread. Father Jose Maria ladled the soup into white ceramic mugs with blue trim. Slowly the mugs were slid around the table until we all had some. Then he said a blessing and we ate mostly in silence, holding the hot cups in our cold hands. I remember how quiet it was, as we all focused on the warm soup; the only sound was the clinking of the spoons on the metal edge of the cups, making music of this communion.

When we were done, Father Jose Maria asked us to sing, and since we were of so many different nations, he led us in "Ode to Joy" singing only "la, la, la" instead of words. It was a wonderful feeling of community, the closest I had felt since our beginning. Then he made a speech, which my friend Iris roughly translated like this: "The Camino is a special walk that inspires people in a new way; I have been serving pilgrims here for over thirty years. They come from all the nations of the world, different politics, different religions, and different views. But not once has there

Serving up the traditional garlic soup

ever been an altercation or an argument among the pilgrims. Because ultimately the Camino is about love—of God and of one another."

So this pilgrimage was about love. How simple. In the midst of my irritations, lack of sleep, and focused energy of getting to the next town, I had forgotten. The pilgrimage was a deep yearning for God, a yearning for community, and a yearning to know and love—even the self—more completely. All my questions about how I'd failed as a pastor and the angst about what was next in my work life, my call, seemed so far away and irrelevant in this gathering of pilgrims; and instead of focusing on all my barriers to closer union with the Divine, I had forgotten this most important truth—it's about Love. Love that was already here, already now, already with us. That was all I needed to know for now. Hadn't I prayed to just "Show Up and Pay Attention"?

After the priest had finished, I helped clean up the cups and silverware, deliver them back to the kitchen, and then wipe the tables.

Again, such simple things and yet they were healing me in a way that surprised me. Peace swept over me, like the peace I'd felt at the first Knights Templar church in Eunate. Was it because I felt useful again? Because this was something familiar to me? With each day so full of new experiences, new faces, and new places, the ritual of clearing the table and washing dishes grounded me. I realized that I liked to serve; I felt like myself again. And thus far, I felt as if I hadn't served anyone except myself. It wasn't a criticism as I thought it, rather an observation. Normally my days would be full of serving. I didn't realize how much I missed it.

Loving to serve didn't feel like something I worked hard to achieve or take credit for. It's the legacy of my family and my years in the church. And it's not that I don't recognize the shadow side of service. I'm enough of a feminist that serving others, particularly as it related to serving meals and cleaning up afterward, is something I resented at times in my life. When serving is a "should" rather than a gift of the heart, the server suffers. But the truest sense of serving puts all things right in my soul. If things are right with God, then you can't help but want to serve others. It assured me that night on the Camino when I cleared the table. God was in me and I in God. I wrote in my journal that night:

I am in a place of passion—the passion of San Juan to serve others seeking God. I know one of the reasons I am on this pilgrimage is to more fully come to my own passion for serving; I can almost see myself, serving in joy—without care for what others think of my way of serving or a need to rescue them. Such a balance this would be for me! What a transformation that would be! I ask for the energy of San Juan then in this place and the knowing that he had of the power of the cosmos in birthing creativity.

What is the "nettle" of this place? The cold—will my bones ever warm up again—and maybe the pain in my hips!

*Re-examine all you have been told in school or church
or any book; dismiss what insults your very soul,
and your flesh shall become a great poem.*

WALT WHITMAN

Chapter 9

Into the City

I remember the dawn over the church as we left San Juan de Ortega. We stopped on a rise leading up into pine forests and turned to see the rosy streaks of sunlight outlining the spire. The remote monastery had been an important stop, deepening my sense of community with other pilgrims. How strange that we would leave this out of the way place in the morning for the frenzy of the big city of Burgos by this afternoon.

The skies looked friendly—some clouds but nothing that looked like a day of rain. We walked into the next village, Ages, and had a wonderful breakfast of apple pastries with café con leche for Steve and tea for me. A few kilometers farther was the UNESCO World Heritage Site of Atapuerca. The prehistoric caves found here contain the earliest human remains ever discovered in Europe. The remains date back eight hundred thousand years, and the ongoing dig has evidence, as yet unconfirmed, of human activity from over one million years ago. The center was closed when we passed, but there was an eerie model of our ancestor, looking like a sophisticated monkey, outside the building. I knew there was ancient history on this pilgrimage, but to try and wrap my mind around human ancestors of one million years ago was not something I could comprehend; I could only walk on, stunned in a new way.

From here on was a gradual climb to Cruceiro, the highest point of the climb that day before dropping down toward Burgos. As we hiked up,

I couldn't help thinking about what I had written in my journal the night before; I'd named that persisting pain in my hips as my "nettle." I could feel that pain with every step, sometimes worse on the right, sometimes worse on the left. I noticed all the piles of rocks along the Camino once again. They had been a constant on this journey. Perhaps originally they had been way markers, but as the tradition of the Camino grew, placing a rock on one of the piles was a way of making prayer—for help, for thanks, for pardon, for a cure. I picked up two rocks as I climbed, and when it felt right, I placed them on a pile of white rocks, indigenous to this area, asking for an easing of pain in my hips.

About an hour later I could see the crest of the hill and the huge wooden cross with a large pile of stones at its base. I had come on this journey, struggling to decide what it meant to be Christian. I always felt there was something more that wanted to come to life, a more inclusive understanding of people, a more transformed way of living.

As G. K. Chesteron wrote in 1910 in his book *Orthodox,* "The Christian ideal has not been tried and found wanting; it has been found difficult and left untried."

My colleague at the church I served had a vision of Christianity as a ministry to the "least, last, lost, and dying." But the church had become so institutionalized that those aspects of ministry were sidebars to the ministry of being comfortable with the status quo, rationalizing our wealth, and upholding tradition over gospel. Could I question Christianity while still dedicating my life to Christ? I added another rock to the huge pile below the cross, and unbidden, I said, "The sacred heart of Jesus." This was a Catholic saying, not a Lutheran one. Often it was drawn with blood dripping from it, a repugnant image to me. *How strange,* I thought.

I walked on maybe fifty yards and turned back to look at the cross. I called it the Cecil B. DeMille moment of my Camino. The clouds had shifted in that way that allowed the sun to shoot down onto the earth in slanting rays, lighting up the background of the cross. I started to laugh out loud at God's sign to me. "Ta da! I'm bigger than all your questions

and doubt. Remember what you just heard the priest at San Juan de Ortega say? The Camino is all about love."

I turned back to the path ahead only to be struck by the surprising form of an old, torn gold-vinyl sofa sitting in the middle of the field without context. Beyond the fact that it was so incongruous, I simply didn't want it to be there marring the beauty and significance of this particular mountaintop. Who had brought it up here and why? What was its purpose?

Since I was seeing relevance in everything as the path unfolded, I let myself just look at it. If all things on the Camino could be there to help reveal more of one's self, I decided that this old sofa represented all the parts of me, and all the parts of others that I don't particularly want to look at. My definition of perfection would not allow the old sofa, but life is both what I judge to be beautiful and ugly, good and bad. Without judgment, it just is.

Perhaps there was a story behind that sofa that I couldn't see. Perhaps it fit in some way, if only to now call attention to my judgment again. How ironic to have that awareness as we headed down the mountain to the big city; the trail led directly by the city dump, bordered by a chain-link fence again woven with straw crosses.

As we entered the suburbs, the heat of the noonday sun bounced off the cement sidewalks. Cars buzzed past us, the air swirling angrily around us as if punching us with gusts. The stench of fumes and the lin-

gering odors of the city dump insulted us as we came to the city limits, the large red sign deftly painted with a wide variety of graffiti.

When a city bus pulled into the parking lot where we were having coffee, it looked like a limousine arriving just for us; we hopped on board, verified it would take us to Burgos Centro, and relaxed for the last few kilometers into the city. We hopped off at the core of the city, buffeted this time by the throngs of people and bikes and baby carriages that pushed down the street in both directions. We negotiated our way over to a large city map to see where we were but couldn't decipher anything. While Steve persisted, I looked in the guidebook for suggested accommodations; hmmm, Hostel Garcia was mentioned. I looked up and right there was the sign for it on the third floor of the building just across the street. Though the beds were a bit saggy, the locks tricky, and the towels thin, it felt like sanctuary. We had a delightful little windowed balcony, with just enough room for two tiny chairs and a table. We washed clothes and hung them in the sun as the crowds streamed by below us, an endless supply of good people-watching.

After resting briefly, we were eager to see the famous Catedral de Santa Maria, another first for Steve. If he had been awed by the country churches, seeing the cathedral nearly overwhelmed him. There are no words for the architecture or carvings, the sculptures, the gold inlay, the paintings, the artifacts, the marble, the soaring domes, the myriad panes of stained glass and rich wooden panels. It took us hours to walk through it, to wrap our eyes around centuries of construction in a variety of styles. Always our eyes were drawn up, up, up. The whole building pointed to heaven, yet it was so grounded on earth. We left the cathedral a little dazed. We sat outside by the fountain and waited in the sun, drunk with images and feelings.

"It is so amazing," said Steve, "just from a construction standpoint." Being a general contractor, this would be his first impression. "But I also wonder about all the money and time that went into it, all the people who had to work for pennies to build it, all those who died

The Burgos Cathedral

building it, and the kings who funded it. Does it feel to you like God wanted that?"

We sat in silence a little more, thinking it over.

"It does seem a little out of sync with the fact that Jesus was born in a stable," I said. Yet I could not deny the feeling of the Holy within this structure. I did not doubt that those masons who built the cathedral or those artisans who filled it with their creations were filled with faith and dedication to God as they did their work. Was this cathedral a monument to the glory of men or the glory of God? Yes, that very paradox of the nature of Jesus—both human and divine. This was the paradox of the cathedral as well.

I was also tickled to see that an old painting of Mary Magdalene was leaning against a wall, which our guide told us had been down in the storeroom of the cathedral for years. It had yet to be hung, but we were told there was an "increasing interest" in the Magdalena. You can't lock up the Feminine Divine forever.

Solvitur ambulando. It is solved by walking.

St. Augustine

Chapter 10

The Meseta Forms Us

Day 13. Burgos to Hornillos: 18.8 km; adjusted for climb: 19.5 km (12 miles)

When we awoke the next morning, we were surprised at the activity for a Sunday, expecting quiet streets, not the hum of early traffic; we had planned to go to an early Mass, have breakfast, and start walking. It was so strange that all the shops were opening up and the vendors opening their stalls. It was a good example of when the mind sees only what it wants to see. Shops don't open up on Sunday, but instead of realizing we were a day off, we thought perhaps it was different in Burgos. However, when the banks opened as well, we found a calendar and realized it was Monday. The journey had worked its magic on us, and we had lost track of days. In retrospect, I realized that the day before was very much a day of worship for me. It was perfect that my mountaintop experience had been on that first day of the week.

Laughing at our mistake, we started out of Burgos and onto the meseta, the flat and hot plain that would take us to the next big city of Leon. It lived up to its name that late morning; the sun was pounding down, and we stopped often for water. We tried to stay disciplined about drinking often, taking vitamin C to ward off colds and glucosamine for our joints every morning, and stopping to cool our feet every hour or two. We planned to go as far as Rabe de las Calzadas by two o'clock, where the guidebook advised there were close to sixty beds. But the reality was this: the first albergue had closed because the owner had health problems and the other albergue had only eight beds. We did arrive as numbers seven and eight, but the owner would not register us until she opened at three o'clock. As we waited, other pilgrims arrived, and at three o'clock we learned that those who had walked the farthest got to come in to be interviewed to see if they were really pilgrims. This woman was so abrupt and militaristic in her style that she was dubbed, the Gestapo Lady. Later we would hear that she was so impassioned that the Camino remain truly a pilgrimage that she set certain rules for her guests. She reportedly served a wonderful meal and was quite attentive to those who had injuries or blisters, applying some healing local mud, which seemed to work wonders. However, we had not walked far enough that day to qualify for her lodging, so once again, we ended up walking farther than we had planned, as if a short day was never our fate.

We felt as if we were swimming in fields of green now—all sorts of cereal crops growing in these impossibly rocky soils. I had to take a

Setting off on the Meseta, the plain of the Camino Frances

picture of the earth as it was so far from the deep black loam of Iowa. And yet, it certainly could be fertile. We loved watching the wind sweep across the wheat in deep caresses. Perhaps because I grew up in Iowa, I didn't mind the mostly flat meseta and could easily see its beauty and peace.

We reached our destination of Hornillos around five o'clock, and we were happy to see a lovely, clear river on the edge of town, where many pilgrims were soaking their feet and writing in travel journals. But as we got closer, we received some news that had come to be quite familiar: the albergue was *completo,* meaning "full."

We had become almost philosophical about this by now, and since it was so hot and the skies clear, we were considering a night out under the stars. But I desperately wanted a shower after the long, hot day on a dusty road. We went into a little shop to buy some chocolate for strength, and when the lady heard we didn't have a place to stay, she pointed across the street to a *casa rurale,* a private home that takes in lodgers. "Perhaps they have a place," she said. And thus our next adventure began.

"It's all about trust," I told myself for the hundredth time as we bounced down a winding one-lane road off into the meseta. We were riding in the back of an olive-green Toyota sedan that had seen many miles. The driver was talking to us in Spanish, trying to get me to understand that he had once lived in LA and worked for Martin Sheen. He kept pointing at himself and saying, "Mi amigo, Marrr-teeeen Sheeeeen." We hoped we were heading to a house that belonged to the mother of the man at the casa rurale. His home was full, but he said, "Do not worry. My mother has a house, and there is room there." It sounded wonderful, and we assumed it was just down the street. "Wait here, someone will come with a car," he said. And so he had. But it wasn't just down the street.

We careened down the road, swerving around corners and through two small villages, and still we weren't there. I began to check my watch. Where were we going? Steve looked at me and smiled, shaking his head. I smiled too. It was a bit strange but it felt wonderful to have someone drive us; we were going to have a place to stay and the evening was beautiful. I practiced trusting.

It was about twenty minutes before we turned down a winding lane, and we saw a huge hacienda in the distance. As we drew near, a cacophony of sound erupted as dogs, geese, ducks, and exotic birds began announcing our arrival. I've used the word *menagerie* loosely before when describing a place with a lot of different animals, but here was the true definition. As our chauffeur took our bags, we crossed a small bridge over a creek. And then we saw that the whole house straddled the creek. Holding ponds had been made for the huge assortment of waterfowl that roamed the place, some of which enjoyed threatening us as we walked by. Two huge Saint Bernards, a hound, a terrier, and a baby fox greeted us. Turkeys, peacocks, pheasants, and plumed ducks circled the yard. Our bags were whisked up to a lavish bedroom, we were shown the shower and told dinner would be at nine o'clock. I was in awe of how we had been provided for that day.

One would think that I would finally be unconcerned after my resolution to trust. But then secondary worries assailed me: would we have enough money to pay for it? As I looked around this exotic place and began to meet the other lodgers, I realized we were in an upscale category of accommodation. We were expecting the usual peregrino albergue. How much would it cost? Why hadn't we asked? Our ATM hadn't worked at the bank we stopped at in Burgos, so we weren't flush with cash, figuring we'd run into another bank but had not. Steve and I began to pool our resources, searching in all the hiding places we used to squirrel away money. We had ninety-eight euros. My gratitude at having a place to stay quickly deteriorated to resentment. Why hadn't the man told us how much it would cost? Or that we would be expected to pay for meals? It wasn't our fault we may not have enough and on and on. The worries tumbled in my brain. What would the owners think of us when we couldn't pay? That we were poor? That we were trying to defraud them? What would the other boarders think? If Hornillos had no bank, where could we get money? What if the ATM didn't work again?

Dinner was at least different from our usual fare. A wonderful squash soup, interesting appetizers of cheese and meats, a mutton dish for the main course. Only dessert was a little disappointing—yogurt. Breakfast the next morning was unremarkable—the usual bocadillos with cheese. I could see others discreetly getting little slips of paper. Oh here it comes, I thought. The moment of decision. How much would it be? And what would I say if it was more than I had? The chauffeur who doubled as the waiter handed me my slip: seventy-eight euros. Whew. Now all my worrying seemed silly; but what will it take to move to a place of being that realizes this from the start? It was so humbling to realize my attachment to money in these ways. Something about money was caught up in my identity and my worth.

I am the generation that has Depression-era grandparents and parents. I still scrape the butter wrapper to get every last bit of butter, just as my grandma did. Both of my parents lost their fathers in 1933, and they were both eight years old at the time. I can't imagine the desperate situation that left their mothers. Both worked varieties of jobs to survive; my father and his siblings had to be separated and went to live with other family members as Grandma Lena couldn't provide for them all. Thus when my father began to make a comfortable living as a farmer himself, he reacted by buying nice clothes and cars and building a new house. He instilled in us, to the point of abuse at times, the importance of working hard to make money. It isn't so easy to chuck all that early training or the value system that says security is money. But the Camino was trying its best.

Confessions: I think it is one of the hardest lessons Jesus taught—you can't serve two masters; it's either money or God. I was on this pilgrimage supposedly in faith, yet in truth, I was trusting money. That verse that Jesus says to his disciples in Matthew 19:23 haunted me: "It is easier for a camel to go through the eye of a needle than for someone who is rich to enter the kingdom of God." I don't think he said that to make me or anyone feel guilty. I think he was just speaking the truth about the human condition—and the transformation that could happen if we had the freedom to sell everything and give it to the poor—as he suggests to this rich man who comes asking about eternal life. I can't judge that rich man in the story who goes away grieving for "he had many possessions." He was me.

Day 14. Hornillos to Castrojeriz: 21.2 km; adjusted for climb: 22.4 km (14 miles)

With twenty euros in our pocket, we headed to our next destination— Castrojeriz, hoping this village of one thousand was big enough to have a bank. The meseta was beautiful that morning with its wide, undulating fields and vast, blue skies. We were peeling off layers of clothes and soon putting on sunscreen as the sun and the pavement cooked us from top to bottom. I loved the town of Hontanas and its welcoming cafés, but we walked on, not knowing if we could spend money yet. We again ate leftovers: slightly stale baguette, stinky cheese, and bruised apples. Fifteen kilometers into our day, we came to Arcos San Anton, an ancient monastery now in ruins. It was once a hospice for peregrinos in the eleventh century and was run by monks of the Antonoine order, affiliated with the work of one of the desert fathers of Egypt, St. Anton. This order's sacred symbol was the Tau cross, looking much like the capital T. The mystical tradition holds that these monks could cure the disease called St. Anthony's fire, a gangrenous skin affliction, by using the Tau cross—Tau meaning "love." There isn't much left standing of this old monastery save a huge arch over the road and an ornately carved door that remains upright. Despite the ruins,

I had a good feeling about this place and could still sense its blessing as we passed under the arch.

We were now in a wide and much flatter part of the meseta. We could easily see Castrojeriz off in the distance and the old castle that dominated the landscape up on a hill above the city. This castle had seen many battles during the reconquista between the Moors and Christians.

My back was in spasm as we walked into town. Despite that, we had settled into a four to five kilometer per hour walk that would be our usual pace for the rest of the Camino. The first albergue was, you guessed it, *completo*. As we made our way to the second one, I noticed a pensión, La Cachava, with a Visa symbol on its window. We had one of those cards with a Visa symbol. It was cool in the foyer; and there was an open room. We took it. Was this God smiling at my worry and providing again?

Pedro, our host, had lived in the United States for many years as an airline consultant. But now in his forties, he and his wife yearned for a simpler lifestyle. They decided to return to Spain, buy this hotel, and live out the dream. He would have time to be a chef and she an artist.

Living a more simple lifestyle. This desire has been our own as well. We had made a start prior to the pilgrimage; we sold our larger home and planned to homeshare with a friend. We traded our SUV for a compact car, and both of us had made career decisions to allow more flexibility in our time. But like Pedro, it isn't easy to really make the switch to a simpler lifestyle when we are certified overachievers and everyone has come to see us that way. It is difficult to learn to say no. I even practiced with Steve as to how to answer a phone call regarding new construction—"I'm not taking on any new work at this time." We used to laugh as he tried it out, but when he got the next phone call, he was able to make it real. I had to make the difficult decision of leaving parish work as I've said before. How would our health insurance work out? How would it be to make less money? Yet as we took these steps, it felt as if we were becoming more of who we were meant to be. Without fully acknowledging it, the decision to walk the Camino was practice in this new lifestyle; certainly we were living simply as we walked. And it was not only in the physical aspects of having two changes of clothes and bunkbed accommodations most of the time, it was also in the flow of the day. All we really had to do was walk, eat, and sleep. The basics. It felt similar to remote backpacking trips in Alaska in that regard—without the intrigue of wild animals.

Castrojeriz was sweet and steep. We wound through its maze of streets and stairs, looking for the one bank in town. You could enter the little ATM nook by sliding your debit card in a slot. Once secured inside, I slipped my debit card in the machine, waiting for the miracle of little colored-paper euros to emerge. It didn't work. We tried Steve's debit card. It didn't work. I noticed a little panic arising inside me. When we tried our credit card instead, out poured the euros; our money belt bulged again, and yes, I confess yet again, it made me so happy.

That evening's dinner was one of the three best of the Camino. A cold tomato soup appetizer, garbanzo bean and sausage soup, thinly sliced Argentinian beef, green salad, and rice pudding. At this meal we met three Canadian brothers in their fifties, who were walking the Camino. All big and strong-willed, each of them said that they came along to keep the other two from fighting. "Mom told me not to let anyone get lost," said the one who had the original idea for the trip. They were taking the day off from walking, as one of them was having foot problems.

It was about here that I began to miss the conversation that occurs between women friends. It's not better, only different than the talking with my husband. To him talking is a necessity but not a real pleasure as it is for me. He tried to fill in the gaps, but it was another aspect of my life that was removed for now, and in hindsight, good for the work of transformation. As an extrovert, I could easily slip into identifying myself by how many friends I have and how they needed me. I wouldn't want to be without these friends in my life, but for the weeks of walking, the silence ripened the time for the work of the soul. Again, as I did in seminary without friends, I had to ask, "Who am I when I'm not trying to please others? Who am I if no one needs me? In this work of simplicity, could I really move from a life of doing to a life of being? And still contribute in this world? What does that look like?"

In our guidebook, the author had his own personal reflection, calling himself "a tamed man addicted to the approval of friends and family, masking the wild man desperate for the freedom that comes with authentic living and dedicated to painting a larger canvas." I starred the words in the book, feeling as if he had mirrored my own deep desires. Maybe I was taking a step up on that spiral staircase of meeting the same issues with a new heart.

Day 15. Castrojeriz to Frómista: 25.5 km; adjusted for climb: 26.7 km (16.7 miles)

It was now May 9, 2007; we had gone about two hundred miles of our five-hundred-mile trip and were right on schedule. I hated to leave the soft bed and down pillows of La Cachava, but the wanderer was in both of us. We were eager to see what each day would bring and what was just over the next hill. In this case, there was one *big* hill on the outside of town that promised to get the blood moving that morning. We had breakfast on the way out of town, eating leftover yogurt and baguettes from our backpacks, anxious to start walking before the sun starting blazing.

From the top, we had a sweeping view of the valley, and we could imagine the many armies that had marched into this area in one battle after another. It was still and warm, and after that first climb, the day would be a flat walk past wind farms and *bodegas* (caves in the hill where wine is kept). Some new crops were being planted, and hay was being mown.

The sound of big tractors and the smell of alfalfa brought back so many memories of growing up. It was both a beautiful and difficult time in my life. If I keep my perspective of a child, I don't think there is anywhere as soft and expansive as an Iowa sunset. And nowhere was the work any harder, longer, and colder. I could not wait to leave the farm and go to college.

Although I still think I was pushed too hard on the farm, I no longer think that my life should have been different from what it was; all of that hard work and determination was making it possible for me to be on this journey across Spain.

We had reserved a room at a hostel in Frómista, but when we arrived, we learned there was room in the much cheaper albergue. We decided to save money and stay there instead. We spent the rest of the afternoon restocking our food supply, washing out clothes, and figuring where we could buy a deck of cards to play cribbage.

Confessions: I complain about how tired I am and how my feet hurt, but it's mostly because I want to push myself along on this journey, just like I was pushed on the farm.

Day 16. Frómista to Carrión de los Condes: 20.1 km (12 miles)

The path was primarily along a clear, running river, and we were bombarded by the music of laughable-sounding frogs, cuckoos, and a myriad of other songbirds. My back was tenuous, and I considered calling a rest day, but once again, Steve took my pack and by going slowly and finding a branch to use as staff, I was able to keep walking.

Passing old canals used long ago to transport grain from the fields to the mills, we came to the town of Carrión de los Condes. I knew the term "carrion." In Alaska we have to be careful in the spring as hiking begins, because hungry bears, just out of their dens, are feeding on the carrion—the remains of animals who haven't made it through the winter. The bears don't like to give up their food anytime, but in spring they are particularly grouchy and protective, so we hike making lots of noise and coming around corners carefully to avoid surprising them—or us.

We learned that this town was the site of severe persecution of Jews and in the late 1300s all the Jews were forcefully baptized as Christians. That is a chapter in church history so contrary to the teachings of Christ that it rattles my bones. And the town is also the site of many bloody battles during the time of Charlemagne—perhaps the reason for the name containing "carrion."

We found not only lodging at the albergue that afternoon but a place for a leisurely lunch and a phone for calling home. The quote for the day in my guidebook was: "I have begun to have an idea of my life . . . as the gradual discovery and growth of a purpose that I did not know—Joanna Field."

Was some purpose gradually growing on this journey that I did not yet see? I was intrigued by that thought and how the Source often works in the dark. I remembered hearing in spiritual direction that God may transform us in ways we are unaware, because it is the most loving way to work. Sometimes there are things in our past too painful to bring to the surface, yet God can still change even these if we so desire. Gerald May proposes in his book *The Dark Night of the Soul* that unlike its usual definition of that time of depression and trial, the dark night of the soul means that time when we can't sense God working, and all we can do is trust. In that, the relationship grows.

Confessions: In hindsight, I can say the back pain kept me very much in the moment as I assessed its changes and accommodated to fit, but at the time, I didn't see any gift in it. It was just another thing that made me vulnerable, uncertain, and uncomfortable.

Day 17. Carrión de los Condes to Terradillos de los Templarios: 26.8 km; adjusted for climb: 27.3 km (17 miles)

This road was like the unrelenting straight roads in Iowa, and the many fields in stages of planting on either side reinforced the resemblance. It was easy to get lost in reverie this morning, having noted before starting that there would be no 90 degree turns to miss if I was lost in thought. It was on this lonely stretch of road that we first met a pilgrim coming from the opposite direction. After these days of following the yellow arrow to Santiago, I had somehow believed this to be a one-way path; of course, it was not. In the early days of the pilgrimage, the peregrinos had to turn around and walk home again. We would catch a plane or bus back to Madrid, but for the first time, I pondered how hard it must have been to know you had hundreds of miles ahead of you yet after reaching the goal of Santiago.

The pilgrim who came toward us was intimidating. Tall, thin, and wearing flowing white robes, the man strode forward with his staff, decorated in shells and feathers. And when he passed, he turned his face to me with a wild, wide-eyed gaze, as if daring me, challenging me, testing me with his look to see if I was worthy of this walk. If he'd been wearing a camel-skin shirt, I'd have believed he was some manifestation of John the Baptist.

Today marked the halfway point of the trip. What a strange mix of elation and regret filled me when I saw the sign. I think for the first time I believed that my back would have its ups and downs, but it wouldn't stop me from walking to Santiago. The regret was feeling as if it was all going too fast. I had a nagging feeling that I should be walking the Camino differently, more reflectively.

We were heading for the town called Terradillos de los Templarios, a humble village without services. It was so called because it was a former stronghold of the Knights Templar. The albergue was named Jacques de Molay, after the last grandmaster of the Order, and huge flags bearing the crest of the Knights Templar were flying overhead. We were early enough to get beds for the night and sign up for the evening communal meal. Then we settled in the sun to read and talk and soak up the residing presence of those ancient knights.

The Knights Templar had fascinated me long before this trip and long before *The DaVinci Code* came out—perhaps because I am attracted to mysticism. But I was also intrigued by their honor code, bravery in battle, and dedication to service. Perhaps the romantic in me wanted to imagine knights on great steeds, defending the innocent pilgrims and living a life of nobler ideals—the same kind of mystique that surrounds the Knights of the Round Table and Camelot. At one time the Knights Templar owned 40 percent of Spain and the many churches and castles across Spain preserved this history. What captivated me most was the fact that this order, which existed for only two centuries and was effectively ended by papal decree in the late fourteenth century, still had avid supporters in the twenty-first. This albergue was only one of several testaments to the continuing devotion of some Spaniards to their history and identity.

One of the things I liked about this albergue is that no one was turned away. Even when the beds all filled up, they offered the dining room floor to late-arriving pilgrims.

The albergue of the famed leader of the Knights Templar

The other delight were the spirited and friendly hosts, who fed us all around crowded tables that night, bantering with the guests, teasing and laughing as the meal was served. And the third delight was an old, spoiled Husky that lolled on the grass, sang for his supper, and reminded me of the three Huskies we have loved in our life in Alaska, so wild in spirit we could never say we "owned" them.

I looked at the register at this albergue as it lay on the counter by the door. I noted that by this count, 75 percent of the pilgrims were German, signing in *Allemagne* under the country column of the sign-in sheet. Again, this awareness of my irritation with Germans. The guidebook had asked, "Will we find the courage today to open our heart and offer love?" I wrote in my journal, "One of my old hatreds has been the German ancestry of my family—its stoicism, alcoholism, and workaholism. Today I've become aware of that old hatred and ask to see the strength of that heritage instead. I am surrounded by Germans! There must be something here to see!"

A Swiss man at my table that night said that there were many subtleties of the Camino that you would miss if you didn't understand Spanish well, hidden levels of mysticism on the road. His Spanish companions had pointed out little signs in unobtrusive places along the way that were written in code or left as messages. Some of them centuries old.

Confessions: I wonder how much I am not seeing that is obvious, let alone hidden. I am so self-absorbed just wanting sleep and relief of back pain.

Day 18. Terradillos de los Templarios to El Burgo Ranero: 29.9 km (18.7 miles)

We thought it would be luxurious to have a room just for three at Terradillos, and the man who joined us in ours was small and fit. I imagined at last I could sleep the night without being awakened by snoring.

Thus I learned to never make assumptions. This man snored louder than anyone to date. I was getting accustomed to folding my pillow over my head to augment the earplugs, but still I heard the *roncar*, Spanish for "snore." As I lay awake, I tried to meditate in time with the snoring, do breathing exercises, or pray. But none of these were as good as sleep. I looked over at Steve and saw that he was awake too. He rolled his eyes as the snoring decibels increased. We decided we might as well rise early and get on the road.

Footlong green lizards, honest-to-God shepherds, and Charlemagne's bloody battlefield were highlights of the trail to El Burgo Ranero. The trail continued very flat, and we now began walking on government-built paths called *sendas* that were intended to help the pilgrim, but our guidebook called them "soul-less."

Absolutely straight and very close to the adjoining road, there was no strolling through the fields as before. Trees had been planted alongside the path but weren't quite big enough yet to offer good shade.

About halfway through the route that day, we saw a band of sheep far out in the field. As we grew closer, we saw three herding dogs keeping the strays in line and a tall lean shepherd with a staff leading the flock. He moved so slowly, letting the flock graze, occasionally stopping to throw a stick for the dogs. When it was time to move, he would call out to the sheep, and in unison they would pick up and follow him across the fields. I had assumed that the dogs would be the drivers, but most of the motion required only the sound of the shepherd's voice. It reminded me of that verse from the Bible when Jesus says, "I know my sheep and my sheep know my voice." I was fascinated at how willingly the sheep followed the shepherd's commands. It appeared that this flock could wander at will; no fences barred the way. There must have been some agreement among the farmers that the sheep could roam, keeping the weeds down. It was an idyllic scene and as the shepherd moved, I could imagine him in a long lineage of shepherds, dating back centuries. His flat, billed cap, ragged woolen cardigan, and dark shirt buttoned up to his neck seemed a picture out of place with the year 2007. I wondered if there would be shepherds to take his place or if they were now a dying breed.

Stopping often to soak our feet in roadside streams kept us cool in the heat of the day. Steve had a tested theory that if we stopped whenever our feet felt hot, we could avoid blisters. So far he'd been right. We never suffered from the many and severe foot ailments of our fellow pilgrims. I once saw a blister two inches wide and eight inches tall up the Achilles tendon of a woman from the Netherlands. She was quite proud of her blister, but I shuddered.

By early afternoon we had arrived in El Burgo Ranero, nearly 30 kilometers. We came upon an albergue where we could have a private room for twenty euros. It seemed a small price to pay for no snoring. We had a late lunch in the Spanish style and then walked around the nearly deserted town. We wandered into the village church and were amused to find an animated conversation going on between the priest and one of the women who was decorating the altar with flowers. She was patiently listening to the priest but obviously set on doing things her own way. When he saw us, he broke off and excitedly told us about the church, most of it wasted on us as he spoke rapidly in Spanish. When we left, he repeatedly kissed me on both cheeks a little too enthusiastically for comfort, and I smelled the strong wine on his breath. The woman looked on in disgust.

By day 18, we knew we were being changed by the journey. We could feel the center of our souls settle into a way of being—quiet, full of awe, open. We were tied deeply to the earth and glad we'd come in springtime; the smell of freshly turned earth and newly mown hay were our constant perfume. New spring flowers continued to entertain us, and the air was crisp and clean. There was also a deepening of our humility as we walked. It was easier here to see our place in the history of man, to hesitate at the monuments and structures that whispered ancient tales and tribulations. Our own relationship grew steadily closer as we depended on each other to share the beauty and the beasts of the trip.

Our patience with each other deepened, and we laughed easily now, even when things didn't go as we planned. I was never exactly carefree, always aware of the challenge of the kilometers and climb for each day on my back, but I was worrying less, able to see that we would always have a place to stay somehow. This practice in trusting was working on me.

Day 19. El Burgo Ranero to Mansilla: 24.5 km (15.3 miles)

This was our last full day before Leon and the end of the meseta. As if to imprint itself in our memories, it served up a wild storm, full of wind and wailing as we crossed the kilometers of plains with little interruption from civilization. I loved the storms here in Spain, reminiscent of the riotous storms on the prairies in Iowa. We could see the black clouds mushrooming toward us, and we futilely picked up our pace, hoping it might pass us by. Within an hour, we were fully suited up in our raingear and had tied down Steve's poncho with a rope around his pack as the horizontal rain pelted us. The howling 65-kilometer-per-hour (40 miles-per-hour) crosswind kept us constantly leaning into it to counteract its desire to push us in the ditch. If it had only been from the back of us, we could have sailed down the path! The rain finally stopped, but wind blew on merrily, puffing up its cheeks and exhaling loud and strong. It did keep the heat off of us but was tiring in its own right. We took fewer breaks now, anxious to get out of the gusts and find a place where we could rest.

We were laughing a lot on this day; we had a strange sense of joy as we walked along, mostly alone the entire day save for an intense Spaniard who charged past us but was then limping when we caught up with him and a Chinese couple who were quietly arguing over something, the wife clearly not as interested in this journey as the husband. She would stop frequently to rub her feet or back and, I analyzed, passively resisted her husband's constant urging to walk faster. We lost track of them along the way.

When we entered Mansilla, we trudged on to the albergue and the crowded reception area. We were surprised to find the room full of people with their shoes off and feet up being treated by a smiling woman. The recipients were in good cheer waiting their turn and the host assured us that we could just go ahead and find a bed and come back later to sign in. We heard from others that this was known as an albergue where the hosts used their healing arts as part of their service to the pilgrims. Their friendliness and the obvious care they had for their guests gave the place an aura of refuge.

It was a massive albergue with a web of rooms on two floors. It was always so good to find an open bunk and make it home for the night, and this was no exception. We curled up to nap and journal when we first arrived. For the most part, the other pilgrims tried to talk quietly or sleep themselves. With notable exceptions, pilgrims were courteous and respectful of each other. My nap that day was interrupted by a conversation that perked up my ears: a couple talking in American English. I looked over to see a thin man with a long ponytail and handkerchief tied around his head and an equally thin woman with wild curly hair. They appeared to be in their fifties, and I guessed they were old hippies or at least had lived at the edge of that lifestyle. I wanted to talk with them, just to take the edge off my homesickness, but I realized they were having a very restrained but tense disagreement about whether to go buy food or not. I sensed this was not the first argument of the trip. I decided to let myself fall into that bliss of deep rest after my 24-kilometer walk.

Day 20. Rest day.

This town was a good place to take a rest day and explore locally. By this time, we had a core group of maybe forty to fifty people who we knew along the trail; we never made great friends, but we had a cohort that we called by name and who were basically on the same schedule as we were.

Having followed each other's progress over the past nineteen days, we couldn't help but notice new alliances and maybe romances blossoming along the Camino. In one town a young man and woman talking in the dorm. In the next town, we saw them having a beer outside a café. Then we saw them walking together on the road. Then we glanced over and the girl laughing a little too long at the boy's comments and he stealing longer looks at her. By Mansilla they were openly holding hands and kissing.

A gorgeous tanned blonde girl had also caught up to us about three albergues back. She made quite a stir among the single men, wearing all white, which complemented her perfect tan and blue eyes. It was entertaining to watch different young men slow up or speed up to walk with her, ask her to have coffee, or even delay their trip to stay on her schedule when she pulled a muscle on the front of her shin. It was like watching a moving soap opera unfold with new episodes every day. Ah, love and what it propels us to do!

No, no, there is no going back;
less and less you are that possibility you were.

WENDELL BERRY

Chapter 11

A Shift of Heart

Day 21. Mansilla to La Virgen del Camino: 25 km (15.5 miles) by bus; La Virgen del Camino to Villa de Mazarife: 15 km (9.3 miles) by foot

It was our guidebook that suggested the route ahead to León would leave the rural paths and follow a busy, noisy, and dangerous route along major highways. The author advised readers to avoid all this and take a bus and "spare a prayer for your fellow pilgrims on foot who you will see trudging their way on main roads." We were reluctant to take a bus again. We already had taken one for 9 kilometers to Navarette and one for 4 kilometers into Burgos. Were we getting lazy? We felt we should keep walking. But that changed when I read to Steve from our guidebook about a question to consider:

Most pilgrims will have committed to travel the whole way by foot, which is highly commendable. If this suggestion to ride the bus into town seems like heresy, it might be useful to ask yourself—Why not? You could more than make up for it by all the alternate routes on the trail. The ego and its obsessive behavioral patterns can be just as limiting as a laissez faire attitude and indifference. As in all things, we endeavor to bring mindfulness to our actions. What is your motivation for this journey, the intention you set out with? Does your decision serve that purpose?

Was our original intention ego-driven? Some of it, yes. I could see it more clearly now that our inner selves were a bit more humble. Sore back and sore feet convinced us to go ahead and take the bus through Leon. As we watched some of our fellow pilgrims trudging toward Leon from the bus as the guidebook described, I looked at Steve and asked if he felt bad not being out there. He turned and looked at me and said, "Not at all!" As we passed the factories and yards, busy streets and shops, we knew it was the right decision for us. We would make enough detours and wrong turns to more than make up the kilometers we rode that day.

Steve wasn't interested in staying in the big city; as he learned in Burgos, the busyness of the city was too jarring after the relative quiet of the Camino. Many peregrinos would take a couple of days here in the city to rest and tour and shop. Some were meeting companions who would walk with them on the final leg to Santiago. It was in León that we felt the first licks of loss. We said goodbye to a couple of Camino friends in León who were going home, to return another year to finish. We felt sad with our first goodbyes, and also an awareness that soon we would have to leave a more significant companion—the Camino itself.

The Camino had gradually become almost a palpable entity to me. I had come to know different sides to its personality; I had seen its beauty and been comfortable in the silence together—always a mark of a good friend. Both Steve and I were curiously addicted to finding those yellow arrows and scallop shell signs as well; it was like playing a continuing game of hide-and-seek as we wound our way across Spain. There was a feeling of being secure on the Camino, despite the superficial problems with lodging. We always knew where we were going; even if we weren't sure why, we always knew what we were doing. We had a definite purpose and goal—to reach Santiago in five weeks. Rarely is life and its purpose as easily defined. With those assurances, we could surrender to what happened each day—days that promised adventure and exploration. We were entering the last phase of our long-planned pilgrimage.

A sample of the signs that would guide us across Spain

The day was bright and sunny, but I was shivering in the 11 degrees Celsius temperature (52 degrees F) and brisk wind as we waited to change buses in Leon. It was one of those days when it was hard to find a place for breakfast and a good cup of café con leche. When the bus dropped us off in La Virgen del Camino, it almost felt as if we had played hooky from the Camino for these few kilometers. It had felt luxurious to ride again and watch the scenery pass so quickly. As we headed out of La Virgen del Camino on the edge of León on foot again, the trail split with one version going along the highway and the other into the countryside. Of course, we chose the countryside route to Mazarife, sharing the road with our Danish friend Iris.

For the first time, we had a choice of albergues in this town. The pilgrim grapevine had whispered that the first place hadn't paid their help, so we passed it by and settled into the soft but adequate bunks of Tia

Pepe's. Iris, Steve, and I had a room to ourselves and a huge clean marble bathroom down the hall. These small luxuries continued to thrill us. By this time hand-washing our clothes in cold water had not been enough. They were clean in a sense, but we needed to find a Laundromat. The smell of sweat permeated the fibers. There were just two small grocery stores where we bought the basics for a light dinner.

That night I pulled the mattress off the bed and slept on the floor as the metal springs of the bed sagged deeply in the middle. The wind banged the wooden shutters on the windows, and a motorcycle raced through town a few times before I fell asleep early. Tomorrow would be a long day as we prepared to leave the lovely meseta behind.

Confessions: I was a jumble of paradox. One minute I wanted this challenging trip to be over and the next, the end was coming too fast. On one hand, the fellow pilgrims inspired me and on the other, I was judging them deficient. I could spiral from joy to despondency with just a shift of pain in my body. I saw this so clearly. Yet I remained this pile of opposites.

Day 22. Villa de Mazarife to Astorga: 30.1 km (18.8 miles)

The cold wind whistled as we left Villa de Mazarife in the early morning, telling each other once again that if this was the United States, there would be mobile coffee stands on the outskirts of all these Camino villages. We were sure they'd make a fortune. We stayed on back roads for most of the morning before finally getting coffee close to eleven o'clock in the town of Villavante. The little café here was decorated with witches of all sorts and sizes. It was my first hint we were getting closer to Celtic country. The day was bright and sunny, and we were still walking with our friend Iris.

Just before crossing the Rio Orbiga, we came to one of the great historical landmarks of the Camino—the Puente de Orbiga. This medieval bridge with its many Roman arches carried us through the Paso Honroso, the roadbed of the bridge, so named for its legend of honor that took place here in 1434. The historical marker recounted the tale of a noble knight, Don Sureo de Quinones, from Leon who was scorned by a beautiful lady. Evidently this was a serious insult to the knight's honor and to regain it, he threw down the gauntlet to any knight who dared to pass as he undertook to defend the bridge and his honor against all comers. (Was it honor or his hurt pride?) At any rate, knights from all over Europe took up the challenge. When Don Suero had broken the lances of three hundred challenging knights in the following month, his honor was felt to be redeemed. (Who set the rules for honor redemption?) He rode on to Santiago with his comrades to give thanks for his freedom from love and the restored honor. Some say when Cervantes heard the tale, it inspired him to write his famous work, *Don Quixote.*

Steve and I standing in front of the Puente de Orbiga

The bridge was the site of many other battles, between Visigoths and Swabians, Christians and Moors. But as we crossed it, it was a peaceful day and only the stones could tell the real stories. We stopped in the town of Hospital de Orbigo, obviously named for its former hospital for pilgrims, and stocked up on food. It was a delightful little town, and in hindsight, I wish we had stopped here and sat in the sun by the river. But as it was only noon and the day was so beautiful, we decided to walk on to Astorga.

There was a stirring of energy on the Camino now with all the pilgrims. As we left the meseta and began climbing some gentle hills, we soon would join with the Camino via Plata coming up from the south. With the Camino routes converging, our sense of closing in on Santiago grew.

We lunched on a lovely idyllic hillside full of wildflowers. If I had come with some vague dream of how the Camino would be, this day fulfilled it. We wandered up gentle hills, through little streams, catching glimpses of Astorga in the distance and the mountain range we would cross the next day. It was a long day, and I fooled myself several times thinking we were almost there, but at last we stumbled into Astorga. Iris was nearly spent.

We found beds in the first albergue. It was cool there, and they had a pool of running water for hot feet, Internet access, and a nice kitchen. We were beginning to relax our guard about finding beds. Maybe as the season eased toward summer, more albergues were opening. We went to an outdoor bar to drink cold beer, sit in the shade, and later indulge ourselves at the many seductive chocolate shops.

For all these auspicious beginnings of the day, it ended badly. I was literally awake all night, sleeping next to the worst snorer of the Camino. I even got up and shook him once, trying to get an hour's snooze or so. But he immediately fell back to snoring within minutes. How could everyone else seem to slumber through that? The next morning I learned most of us hadn't. When I met eyes with other pilgrims as we arose, they grinned, shook their heads, and pointed at the man who was still snoring. We'd all had a bad night.

Confessions: I didn't take my sleepless night as good-naturedly as these others; I was having an interior tantrum that he slept so well without apparent concern for others. I could find no charity in my heart.

All about the feet!

Cead Mile failte.
(One hundred thousand welcomes.)

CELTIC SAYING

Chapter 12

Higher Ground

Day 23. Astorga to Foncebadón: 27.2 km; adjusted for climb: 29.2 km (18.25 miles)

Probably because I was so tired, I was less than kind the next day. If my competitive spirit had been simmering all along, today it boiled. I didn't want anyone to pass me on the trail; I was particularly irritated with some old Frenchmen who wouldn't let me by. I was certainly not walking in a relaxed manner. By the time we were in Gaspon 12 kilometers later, only two hours had passed. We were on a 6 kilometer per hour pace, and that was going uphill. We were now ascending the second mountain range and would reach a height of 5,000 feet.

Realizing then how fast we'd been walking, we diverted off the path to sit on the benches outside an ancient church. We rested our feet and ate finger food out of our packs, splurging with lots of chocolate after that fast walk. Our destination for the day could have been Rabanal, but again we arrived so early in the day, we were reluctant to stop. It was only eleven o'clock, yet we had already walked 21 kilometers.

Rabanal was well known for its particular hospitality to pilgrims. I found an excellent Internet connection in a little bar, and the woman behind the counter helped me call ahead to Foncebadón. We decided we had better make a reservation at the Hostal Convento there rather than risk a full albergue in that remote spot. Foncebadón was really only a village of ruins, save for the hostel and albergue and some sheep pens; there wouldn't be a lot of alternatives. And after my sleepless night, I was eager to ensure a quiet night away from the snorers. It was a high point when I actually got through and was able to be understood enough to make the reservation. All that study in Spanish paid off.

The hike up from Rabanal to Foncebadón was about 6 kilometers. To me, it was a sweet dream. My back didn't hurt, the day was clear and beautiful, the temperature perfect, and the hillsides a bouquet of purple and white bushes and flowers. It was the closest I'd felt to a hike in Alaska; I was feeling at home in both body and mind.

Maybe the fact that we had been walking on flat land for the past eight to nine days increased my pleasure at climbing again. Even though it's harder work on the lungs and heart, I've always enjoyed climbing up. I like the sensation of feeling my body working, the quadriceps tightening and releasing, the calf muscles pushing, the body adjusting to the challenge. Perhaps it's the awareness of the breath going in and out so forcibly that reminds me I'm truly alive. Or watching how the attitude of the mind forms the pace and nature of the climbing. I'd learned long ago that there is a way of climbing that seems to conform to the mountain. If you push it too hard, it pushes back. But if your body meets it gracefully, the mountain responds. It's a mystical thing I suppose but also very real. If I force my way through the low scrub, it will tangle and trip me. If I move through it with awareness, I can almost watch it part and allow me through. When I receive the incline of the mountain as a gift, I see beauty everywhere, and I walk in a way that is a perfect balance between the ability of my body and the incline of the slope. My breath is deep and steady, the grip on my shoes solid. But if I hurry, my foot slips and my breath is short or gasping. Ever since I first climbed a mountain, I have never really felt it was a separate thing from my body. And sometimes when I look at the outline of a mountain against sky, seeing its curves and slopes, I imagine myself lying on my side, my head tucked under one arm, draped down the slope. Climbing this mountain brought me back to my breath and my body.

We could see Astorga in the far distance as we made our ascent. About halfway up there was a big cement watering trough full of cold and clear running water. We soaked our feet and legs here while talking with a pleasant English couple and their daughter. They were walking in white pants and shirts with wide-brimmed hats as if on a stroll in the English countryside. It was possible that they had been let out by car to hike this last portion and would meet their ride farther up the mountain. I couldn't imagine they were pilgrims. Wearing my wrinkled and worn zip-off pants and an equally stained shirt, I yearned for a new set of clothes that smelled like something other than a combination of sweat and dirt. I had a strange desire to wear something white.

When we reached Foncebadón, I first thought it looked like a pile of rubble. The rocks of the region lend themselves to being fashioned into walls and fences. Sometime in the past, several huts had lined a vague street. Now they were mostly fallen in, save for the restored convent, which was the hostel, a small church, and the albergue. Lambs, separated from their mothers, bleated from behind a wall of stones. Flocks of sheep wandered the town, watched by a menagerie of huge dogs. Although the dogs were astute at keeping away other stray dogs, they let the sheep wander out onto the paved road without a care, causing many passing cars and trucks to slam on their brakes and sound the horn. We checked into our hostel after negotiating our way past a pair of protective geese who hissed. We were happily surprised to get tasty meatballs and peasant soup for lunch.

Like every veteran pilgrim, we washed out our wool socks first and put them out the window to dry in the afternoon sun. After a hot shower, more handwashing of underwear and shirts, and then a nap, there seemed nothing to do but go for a walk. We wandered up on a cow path into the hills, fascinated by the flowers and the sounds of sheep, cows, dogs, birds, geese, and people. The little albergue was packed with friendly pilgrims and a garrulous host who insisted on cooking lunch for everyone. After this late, big lunch, we snacked that night on pack fare and got a good night's sleep.

The ruins of Foncebadón

Confessions: I indicted myself as an imposter pilgrim. Just as I thought I was walking in a more "relaxed manner," I had walked faster and more competitively than ever. Would I ever learn these repeated lessons of the Camino, especially the first commandment—"The Camino is not a marathon." It seemed that I wasn't taking any steps up on that spiral staircase of awareness.

Day 24. Foncebadón to Ponferrada: 28 km; adjusted for climb:
31 km (19.3 miles) (150 miles to Santiago)

The day's hike took us up another 100 meters to the Cruz de Ferro, the highest point of this mountain range. Here we were surprised to find a huge pile of stones leading up to the simple cross atop a long pole. Evidently many pilgrims bring something from home to leave at this very spot. There were postcards, boots, shirts, pieces of underwear, pictures, licenses, ID cards, jewelry, and messages tied, taped, or stapled to the pole. I had only three large white quartz rocks that I had picked up to set on the pile for friends back home. I wished them clarity, creativity, fertility—each according to a struggle they were facing. At least those were the words that came when I set them down. It was busy around the cross with much picture taking and laughing and talking. I waited for a quiet moment, but pilgrims kept coming in a steady stream, so we walked on through the mountain meadows and grazing cows along the ridge of the mountain.

I didn't want to leave this mountaintop and the vistas spreading out in waves of purple for miles and miles. We sat down often to try and extend our time there, munching apples and talking with other pilgrims about their journey. There were many women walking alone, one an executive from a company in Toronto who was spending her vacation in this way. We walked by the funky little settlement of Manjarin, where facilities were very primitive and from reports, a mix of back-to-nature living and Gregorian chanting. One pilgrim called it the *real* Camino albergue, while another was scornful of the way the host treated the guests. It showed us again that we all experience things so differently and hold onto our opinions like creeds. There is value in holding opinions lightly. It not only lets me enjoy life more but it keeps me in relationship with others.

Finally we began the steep descent into Acebo, marked in the guidebook as *Vigilante!*, meaning to take heed, to be vigilant as we walked down the steep path. It was so much gentler than most slopes in Alaska that Steve and I joked about what word they would use for those slopes. The main worry was avoiding the bikes that blasted down the trail. They could have taken the road, but some wanted the true mountain bike experience. The trouble was, we couldn't hear them coming, and many wouldn't make a sound until they were nearly upon you. Despite that, they were friendly and having a wonderful adrenaline rush. However, we

noted that in the cemetery in the village at the bottom of the slope, there was a modern sculpture of a bicycle in memoriam to a biking pilgrim who died in an accident on that slope.

This village, Acebo, was another place we could have stayed for a while. It was friendly and quiet with a wonderful view on all sides. But again it was before noon when we reached it, and our bodies had literally become addicted to walking. It may just have been our personalities, but just sitting all afternoon seemed less appealing than seeing what was next. The winding trail down by the creek looked so inviting that we headed out again on this hot and humid day to Molinaseca.

Here we made a serious error. There were many hostels and albuerges where we could have rested out of the sun. But Ponferrada was only 7 kilometers away. We could easily make it in another two hours. We took a wrong turn in the outskirts and should have gone the shorter way through the city. As it was, we got caught on a path for a long stretch of hot and dry walking with no water. Then my back spasmed seriously, and I had to lie on the ground for a while in the tiny bit of shade by a garage. Steve took my pack, and we eventually walked on to an open bar. What a welcome sight!

We drank glass after glass of water and ate oranges until we felt rehydrated. The temperatures had soared to 30 degrees C (86 degrees F) and the pavement was hot. We crossed the river and trudged toward the magnificent Castillo de los Templarios—Castle of the Knights Templar.

It was a storybook castle, just as I had drawn them as a child, with high spires, a serrated wall, a moat, and a drawbridge. Bright flags flew from the spires, and tiny windows lined the visage. It was huge both in length and height and had been under reconstruction for over thirty years. I was sure it was full of secret passages and huge banquet halls lined with armor.

The castle of the Knights Templar of Ponferrada was originally a hill fort and later a Roman citadel. At the beginning of the twelfth century, the Knights Templar took possession of the fortress and reinforced and extended it to use it as a palace and as protection for the pilgrims.

We got a room in a hostel for forty dollars with a view of the castle and a TV with an English news channel. For the first time in over three weeks, we caught up on the world news as we washed out clothes, soaked in a bath, and I coaxed my back out of spasm.

By sitting in the square in late afternoon, a pilgrim could usually meet up with other pilgrims—some we knew and some we didn't. It was never hard to spot the pilgrims. The rest of Spain dressed up for the evening parade around the plaza, promenading with strollers and baby carriages, couples walking hand in hand, or teenagers out to impress. Pilgrims had a certain haggard look about them, a map in one hand, scuffed hiking boots, taped knees or ankles, and a pack on their back, maybe a staff in their hand. If they had changed into sandals, the sunburned legs with white feet was a dead giveaway.

I wrote in my journal at this point in the pilgrimage:

Sometimes I have to remind myself I am in Spain. It's not that I could be anywhere, for the country is unique and not like a place I've been before. Sometimes it's only that I do not want to put a name to the place I am—to let this road be anywhere, giving peace and contentment in an unexplained way, inviting the traveler back to an awareness of their spiritual mystery and magnificence. I don't want to name the Camino as being anywhere save where and when a person needs it to be. That sounds mystical perhaps, yet the more I walk this road, the more aware I am that the Camino offers place and space to a homecoming of the spirit; yes, fed by the art and faith and tradition of those before, but it is not so meaningful to me that I come to the tomb of St. James, as it is that I open any place entombed in me.

Day 25. A Rest Day, Almost

We met up with another pilgrim who had rented a car to go see one of the UNESCO World Heritage Sites of old Roman gold mines not far from Ponferrada, where we hiked around the ruins and heard horrific stories of the work the slaves were forced to do to produce the gold. With the evening walk around town, we probably only walked 6.4 kilometers.

Day 26. Ponferrada to Villafranca del Bierzo: 23.7 km (14.8 miles)

My back was feeling better by day two of rest, and we were off again on the Way of St. James, finding our early morning café for coffee and tea. The road climbed as we walked past orchards bursting with figs, cherries, pears, and almonds. We stopped to buy fresh cherries right off the tree, happy with this further sign of spring. We chatted with a young woman who had been living in Colombia teaching English for the past five years after losing both her parents while in college. When I mentioned I was a grief counselor as part of my position, she talked more about losing them, and I realized that her walk was a journey of grief, and she was still trying to find meaning and hope from their early deaths.

We arrived early in Villafranca del Bierzo, which I remember for three significant things: the place where we had the bad midday meal, the relentless hailstorm, and the ceremony of the *Queimada*, or the calling of the spirits. We found our bunks in the old albergue, Ave Fenix, which would transport packs up the mountain the next day for one euro each—a new perk on this trip for us.

I napped and snacked until 10:00 p.m. when it was rumored that Jesus, the hospitalero, would preside at a *Queimada* in the reception area. The guidebook said the *Queimada* was a calling of the spirits—others said the witches, and others said demons. In any case, they were to be called and burned in the fire. Steve couldn't be bothered with what sounded like foolishness to him and fell asleep early. But I, always interested in spiritual practices, was intrigued and stayed up with most of the rest of the pilgrims, writing in my journal and watching the sunset turn purple on the horizon. The air was washed fresh and still felt slightly electric as if the flashes of lightning from the earlier hailstorm that afternoon still sizzled. At last Jesus called us into the patio area, when the sky turned dark, waiting patiently as about forty of us crowded around a small table set in the middle. A huge bowl sat on the table with a large ladle beside it and some small jars.

Through a translator, Jesus asked that we take no pictures during the actual ceremony, but we would have an opportunity afterward. The actual liquid used in the ceremony is made by burning aguardiente, or orujo, a very strong liqueur, with sugar, fruit, or coffee beans. Jesus used a starter from prior Queimadas going back fifty years and growing in potency. It reminded me of how, in Alaska, we save a bit of sourdough each time to begin the next batch of pancakes. Obviously, Jesus had done this ceremony often and enjoyed being the showman.

The lights were turned off, and we became quiet. He announced that it was now time to call the spirits and began a little incantation of some sort that was not translated. He stirred the liquid in the bowl and then ladled up, lighting the liquid in the ladle until it glowed with a licking blue flame. When he lowered it into the bowl, the surface caught fire as well, and then he coaxed the fire until he could lift the ladle several feet above the bowl with the flames swirling up from bowl to ladle, as we joined him in the chant, half laughing, half in awe. Rather than calling on the spirits of the witches, Jesus called upon the past spirits of all pilgrims to heal and protect us. Our voices raised up and down with the chant, and even though it seemed to be mostly in jest, hearing our voices in the dark with the flame spiraling above the bowl was mesmerizing. At last the bowl was covered, and the lights were turned back on.

The translator was quick to explain after the ceremony ended that this was an ancient pagan ceremony and that they only did it for fun. But as he said it, I saw a flicker of anger or surprise cross the face of a woman who was standing behind him and who worked at the albergue. I wasn't so certain she felt the same way about the ceremony. I think, for some, it truly is a calling of the witches and a settling of the demons.

It reminded me of the time we were hiking in the Philippines. Our guide was leading us down a steep mountain trail when suddenly he had us stop and crouch, cautioning us not to move. We obeyed instantly, wondering what danger he saw. Then he pointed to an eagle in the sky, warning that if it saw us, it could take our soul. Then he said casually, "It's just a superstition, but it's true."

Trays of small cups without handles were brought in and each cup was filled with the liquid from the bowl and passed around the circle. No one was to drink until all had a cup in their hands. Then together, at Jesus's command, we all drank together. "Another form of communion," I thought as I sipped the strong brew, tasting of course like liquor, coffee, and sugar.

Jesus, the hospitelero, calling the spirits at the Queimada

Day 27. Villafranca de Bierzo to Ruitelán: 21.1 km; adjusted for climb: 23.2 km (14.6 miles)

Although most of the path was alongside a paved mountain road, there were few cars. A clear river paralleled our walk. By now I had tied a long scarf around my low back like a brace as it felt so unstable. But as I walked, it felt slowly better, and I marveled again how I could keep going the 19.3 kilometers uphill. I felt more at home now, the mountains rising on both sides of the road, full of interesting rocks and flora, the river murmuring beside us, and trees in spring bloom. We reached our destination by one o'clock and joined a queue of pilgrims at the albergue where our pack, we hoped, had been dropped off for us.

It was, as always, an anxious moment to see if beds were available; the hospitalero was slow in checking everyone in, but only so because he was enjoying joking with the young girls, teasing the men, and taking calls on his cell phone. He took each person up individually to see the dormitory, the staircase so small our shoulders rubbed on both sides. But we had a bunk, even a lower bunk, where we could rest our heads. Even more gratifying was the fact that just as we stretched out, it started to rain, big drops splashing against the windowpane. Ah, our timing had been perfect. And there were our packs, waiting for us in the dorm, just as promised.

Other pilgrims were not as fortunate, and they slowly straggled in wet and weary. We had met one of these groups the night before at our albergue. They were friends from England—six of them, in their late fifties. We learned that the leaders were two sisters who had already done two legs of the Camino. The first year was St. Jean to Burgos, the next was Burgos to León, and this year would be León to Santiago. They were long-legged and in good shape, walking fast on the trail. They had somewhat impulsively invited along four other friends who weren't as fit. And one of the group had only lost her husband two weeks prior. By the time they'd climbed the mountain that day, the other four were hurting. To make matters worse, the widow's pack had been delivered to the top of the mountain by mistake, leaving her with no clothes to change into. She was limping badly, and I offered to take a look at her leg, knowing full well it was tendonitis. She'd had only a day's notice that she would be coming on the trip with her friend and only had her old tennis shoes and inadequate raingear.

As I massaged and gently stretched her ankle and lower leg, I again felt more like myself, as I had clearing tables at St. John of the Nettle. I had spent twenty-five years doing this sort of thing as a physical therapist. It happened that I had a spare set of orthotics for shoes with me that fit her shoes, and we got some ice to cool down the inflammation. While I worked on her, she began to tell me the story of her husband and his death. She had come on the trip because she hoped she could grieve as she walked and be supported in the company of friends. Like many long-term caregivers for spouses, she felt guilty that she hadn't been more patient with him. But I reassured her that most caregivers get tired, and to try and remember all that she had done for him. Grief counseling also made me feel like myself; while most of the Camino was unpredictable, I knew how to listen to someone grieving. I was aware that as I gave to her, she was giving to me.

The value of listening was something deeply ingrained in my way of being. I had always loved sitting near elders listening to stories. And as a physical therapist I often gained the trust of patients I saw repeatedly, hearing the stories of pain and struggle beyond the physical pain I was treating. I was already a spiritual seeker as well, and a friend encouraged me to begin seeing a spiritual director in 1992. The title was misleading as this woman was careful not to direct anything, but she would listen with such attention that I would begin to hear my own wisdom, my own direction of the spirit. It was so affirming that I trained as a spiritual director when in seminary and began being with people as a companion on their own journey. By the time I started the Camino, I was listening with a dozen or so people. Listening is so simple but so rare, so profound in its ability to transform. As well as treating her foot, I hoped the listening would treat the grief and guilt she was carrying. We talked for a long time as we waited to be called for dinner that night.

We learned from other pilgrims at this hostel who could translate for us that our host had once run a very successful restaurant in southern Spain, but he hadn't been fully satisfied. When he was introduced to the Camino, he decided he would care for pilgrims as generations of Spaniards before him had done. Beyond his friendly welcome, he provided massage services for pilgrims at the albergue and believed that people are nourished both body and soul by a good meal. He would serve us a community meal tonight.

The doors to the dining room were shut until he was ready. The table had been laid with settings and candles, and as we took our seats, I realized how long it had been since I had had the pleasure of someone taking care of me in this way. We waited as the dishes were brought out—huge bowls of spaghetti carbonara, baskets of bread, and carafes of wine and water. Our host placed them precisely on the table, fussing with the arrangement until he was satisfied. Then with a huge smile on his face, he blessed us and bid us eat.

Conversation swirled around us in Italian, French, Spanish, and German with some English now and then for our sake. As we all struggled for words to communicate, our hands flying to mime what we couldn't say, I realized that this was the real language of the Camino—a blend of all languages with the intention of understanding and being understood, even though difficult. It was called "Caminoese," but underneath it was the language of common humanity.

Day 28. Ruitelán to Fonfría: 22.2 km plus a 4-km detour for 26.2 km; adjusted for climb: 30.3 km. (18.9 miles)

I could title the first part of this day "Lost in the Fog" and the latter "Celtic Celebration." It was a day that began in discouragement and surged to delight. We climbed on the steepest incline of the Camino toward a town called O'Cebreiro, high in the mountains of the province called Galicia. We were now in the thick of Celtic country and even the signs were spelled differently, with x's replacing other consonants in words.

I've long felt a spiritual sisterhood with the Celtic tradition, one that is recorded as early at the eighth century BCE across northern Europe. Much of the culture was destroyed by Roman conquest, but it survived in the island nations of Britain and Ireland, where the customs are still evident today. The Celtic tradition was made up of many tribes, and

A satisfied table of pilgrims after a hearty dinner together

one that also survived was the tribe of Galatians whose descendants are clustered in the northwest corner of Spain in the area of Galicia. The Celtic way was a pagan culture, much assimilated in the Christian tradition but has retained its deep connection to nature, music, dance, myths, mystery, and superstition.

We had been forewarned about the mists of Galicia, but that morning it wasn't mist; it was full-on rain as we started our ascent along the winding mountain road. With the guidebook buried under Steve's poncho and the rain pouring down, I didn't take the time to consult it, and we missed the turn to the path over the mountain. Instead we stayed on the highway, going 4 kilometers out of our way. Once we figured out our mistake, it was too late to go back.

Despite our raingear, we were wet and cold from sweating and discouraged with the detour. We commiserated with another pilgrim who had lost the way and a Camino biker who was having trouble keeping his hands warm. The road didn't have shoulders and cars flew around the corners, forcing us to dive for the ditches more than a few times. It seemed we would never arrive at O'Cebreiro, and I wondered if we had taken yet another wrong turn. Then an old angel appeared. Really he was just an old man filling his water jugs from a spigot that flowed out the side of the mountain. We stopped to ask if we were close to the town. He nodded and looked at us sympathetically. Then he nodded to our water bottles and filled them for us, encouraging us with words we couldn't understand, yet we felt his kindness deeply.

The sign for O'Cebreiro finally appeared out of a thick mist that kept visibility down to just a few feet. High stone walls materialized out of nothingness and then whole buildings emerged. As we walked into the heart of the village, I heard Celtic music playing from a little shop full of jewelry, witches, and other Celtic bric-a-brac. It was like a siren song luring me inside. But hunger was more seductive, and the lights in a little subterranean café across the cobblestone street drew us in. We shed our soggy backpacks and raingear outside the door and then brought them in to dry in a corner. It was so humbling to watch how easily my spirits were transformed by warmth, food, and a dry place to sit down. We munched on huge bocadillos with scrambled eggs and hot drinks. More wet pilgrims were clamoring in after us, and I felt encouraged that we weren't the only ones who had seemed a bit desperate to find the café that morning.

Wanting to make room for others, we packed up reluctantly. It would have been easy to linger there and shop. I bought two pairs of earrings with Celtic designs, a little unnerved by the huge stuffed witches that

Steve and a new friend in the mists of O'Cebreiro

hung down over the head of the cashier as I paid. Save for the Good Witch in the *Wizard of Oz*, witches have had a very negative connotation for me. It was strange to see them so celebrated here. Particularly in Galicia, the *meigas*, or "witches," are steeped in the folklore of the region. The witches in here are deemed to be more benevolent than most. It was a common response to hear when asking about witches in Galicia to be told, "I don't believe in witches, but they are here."

The albergue at O'Cebreiro was closed for renovation, so there was no option but to keep walking. It must be a beautiful place in the rare days of sunlight, but in the thick, dripping fog, it remained wrapped. At least now it would be all downhill for the rest of the day.

As we descended, the fog lifted a little, and we caught glimpses of the typical Galician culture—small fields hemmed by mossy stone walls, weathered wooden gates, lush pastures grazed by cattle and sheep. We passed pens of chickens, pigs, geese, and ducks. As we entered the village of Fonfria, we had to flatten ourselves against the fence as huge, plodding milk cows passed by, herded by women with wild red hair. I had to wonder if they were some those benevolent witches.

We passed an open door where ten-gallon vats of milk sat on top of stoves, the thick cream foamy on top. I had a momentary impulse to dip my finger into that cream and take a taste. This was one of the prevailing memories from my own farm childhood. We milked three cows by hand every morning and night. It was the kids' job to carry the stainless steel pails of milk into the well house to keep it cool. There we ran it through the separator, fitting in the filter at the bottom. Then we would slowly pour the milk through to the metal cans that would be taken to market. But some of the milk ended up in our kitchen with a full two inches of cream on top. No one discouraged us from licking the cream back then. We worked too hard to put on weight with it. We didn't churn butter as the generation before had done, but the wooden churner sat in the shed out back. There in Galicia, it was still a way of life. In fact, much of the culture here reminded me of farm culture in the 1950s in Iowa—minus the mountains of course.

We gingerly stepped around a plethora of fresh cow pies lying in the road, and we crossed our fingers as we entered into the new albergue in Fonfria. We were about six pilgrims back in line, and I could see the hospitalero checking off the open bunks. But again there was room for us. Two top bunks, side by side, a modern bathroom, a big heater in the attached garage for drying shoes, clothes, and tents, and ah, a washer and dryer.

By this time, our clothes reeked, despite the daily handwashing. There had been washers and dryers at a couple of other albergues, but either they had been full or I didn't have enough time to wait. Now I made it top priority, and by late afternoon we had warm, clean clothes. In the midst of this, there was an international effort to get my walking sandals down to the albergue from the top of the mountain where I had left them in the café when we had hurriedly packed. With the help of my English friends who spoke Spanish, the barmaid, and Irish guy, we finally got the phone call to the right place and the right person who had found them. Soon a taxi delivered them to the door, and we all cheered, much to the amazement of the driver who shrugged and accepted the nice tip—not usually given in Spain.

Dinner that night was a true celebration. The family who ran the albergue also ran a restaurant across the road and routinely served family-style meals for the pilgrims. I heard some complain about how the villagers were taking advantage of the Camino and commercializing it by doing so, but I didn't see it this way at all. I was so grateful that we could have a good meal provided for us. And above that, the way we were served felt like I was being honored, not used.

About seven o'clock we all marched over the small road below the albergue and into a round building with a conical thatched roof. Inside, a large table curved around at the ends to hold the fifty something of us for a sit-down meal. Clattering sounds rang from the kitchen, and soon three strong, robust-looking women came bearing platters of food and placed them before us with attitude. It was apparent they loved to tease and please. Unlike most meals that were predictable with two plates and then a dessert, this meal just had more food and more food. We started with the hearty soup of the region, *caldo gallego*, and hearty bread. Before we had finished, bowls of penne pasta in tomato sauce appeared, salad, and then chunks of beef and steaming platters of potatoes. We all began to groan with pleasure at the abundant food. The man sitting across the table from Steve, pushed out his belly until it looked like a soccer ball and made everyone laugh when he said, "My wife will never believe I have really been walking 15 miles a day." The atmosphere became more and more merry, and I had to laugh just at the effort everyone was making to tell a joke but have it understood in ten different languages. After a while, no one cared. We just laughed, and it satisfied something deep in my belly.

During the dessert, which was a heavy almond paste-like torte, the Frenchman opposite us remarked that this Sunday would be Whitsunday, and he said it was possible to make it to Santiago in time for the big Mass that day. I realized then that he meant Pentecost. I had totally lost track of the liturgical calendar that divides the Christian year into seasons. But when I counted back to Easter, I realized he must be right. It had been fifty days. It would be Pentecost on Sunday, six days and 151 kilometers, or about 90 miles away. If we kept on our 15 miles (24 km) per day schedule, we would arrive exactly on the festival that marks the coming of the Holy Spirit. It was almost too perfect—to arrive in Santiago at one of the great religious festivals, to end this spiritual journey on a Sunday—my holy day, to be celebrating the coming of the Holy Spirit to people from all lands while in a community from all lands; could it really end in this synchronistic way? Too perfect to be true. I shouldn't have that expectation. It would be counter to allowing whatever happened on the Camino to unfold day by day. It was that night that I began to feel the physical presence of Santiago. How would I enter?

Confessions: Although I was saying I would let it go, the seed had been planted, and I knew I would always be aware that Pentecost was the coming Sunday. I wanted that perfection and would make it happen.

Take me home, Lord; guide me
to the place of perfect repose.

PSALM 84

Chapter 13

Santiago in Sight

Day 29. Fonfria to Sarria: 19 km (11.8 miles)

It seemed as if everything began to ease as we headed downhill the next morning. The mists lifted, the sun came out, and a whole panorama of Galician countryside splayed out before us in the broad valley below. Bushes bloomed by the roadside, birds were singing, and our bodies felt rested and well-nourished from the night just past. I remember the walk down to Triacastela as magical. I was so lost in thought at one point, that I missed a yellow arrow and nearly walked into a herd of oncoming cows until Steve and other pilgrims yelled at me, laughing.

Triacastela means "three castles," and as we wound into town down a steep, muddy path, we could see the remains of two of them on the hillside. We rested at a roadside café there, feeling more relaxed and present. We decided not to take the long way via Samos on our way to Sarria as the day was growing hot, and I didn't want to push my luck with my back. We arrived early in the afternoon to this town of twelve thousand, busy as most towns were with much new construction. We crossed the clear Rio Sarria and climbed the ancient granite steps called Escalinata Maior into the old city of Sarria. Just as we turned the corner at the top of the steps, sweating and thirsty, a man convinced us to take a look at a room above the corner café. We were leery, but as it turned out, it was a great private room for ten euros, and the café would transport our bag to the next town.

Sarria marks the town where many pilgrims begin their trip. The minimum requirement to receive a certificate of completion from the pilgrim office is 100 kilometers. Sarria is 117 kilometers from Santiago, and the closest town to that mark, so many begin here. We spent much of the afternoon and early evening sitting outside a café by the river people-watching. My feet never really stopped hurting by this point in the trip. They were almost constantly sore in some way, yet it was hard to just rest them when I was in a new village or town. There were always interesting things to see and absorb. We had worried about the noise from the bar below our room and being close to the main stairs into the old city, but the night was quiet and we slept well.

Day 30. Sarria to Portomarin: 22.9 km; adjusted for climb: 24.4 km (15.25 miles)

We started out in a light rain. It was amusing to watch all the other pilgrims decide as we did when to finally believe the rain was serious and take the time to put on raingear. When we all finally gave in, took off our packs, wrestled on the ponchos and jackets, the rain quit within ten minutes. But not before we saw a beautiful rainbow span the field ahead of us. "Con Dios," whispered the woman walking along by us. "With God." As we walked along a low stone wall, we began to see old cement stones with the kilometers to Santiago engraved on them, now marking almost every kilometer until we would reach our destination. We stopped and took a picture at the 100 kilometer mark. A pair of worn out tennis shoes were propped on top of the marker as well.

Confessions: Physically, I am tired and ready to be done. But I am more and more reluctant to end this journey in the spiritual sense. It seems all my times of worry and impatience are coming back to haunt me, to shame me, to judge me. I should have done this walk as I vowed—"in a relaxed manner." Could the last 100 kilometers make up for it?

*Looking as worn as these old boots as we neared
the end of the Camino*

*Day 31. Portomarin to Palas de Rei: 26.1 km; adjusted for climb: 28.3 km
(17.7 miles)*

We climbed twelve hundred feet today, but the countryside is beginning to blur a little. Kilometer after kilometer of stone-walled fields, sheep grazing, rock houses, and granaries. These granaries look like little mausoleums at first. Sitting six feet off the ground to keep out the rodents, they are about the size of a large casket, and certainly nothing like the huge granaries that I grew up with.

We had a beautiful little lunch on the side of the road amid lots of wildflowers on this sunny day. The temperature was perfect, and I was again glad we'd come in the spring. I started to take pictures of some of our fellow pilgrims, realizing that it was possible we wouldn't meet up again. We splurged on a twenty-five euro private room in Palas de Rei and lounged in the big central plaza with other pilgrims, telling stories of our journey and laughing now at all our misadventures along the way. Again, we were all feeling the end approaching.

Confessions: My hips and feet are in constant pain. I want to stay and enjoy these last few days moment by moment, but I find myself dreaming more and more of just being done.

Day 32. Palas de Rei to Arzúa: 29.4 km (18.4 miles)

Again we were able to send my pack ahead. I hadn't been able to carry it now for five days, but I now knew I would make it to Santiago. Rain threatened the entire day, but we walked on dry and cool. We entered this town from up above and walked down through its winding streets, stopping in a small chapel to rest. We found a pensión on the third floor of a modern building and, as usual, napped and then went for an evening walk. By now we knew we would likely enter Santiago on Pentecost Sunday, and we talked about how we would do it. Would we go to the big cathedral or find a small one? Would the crowds be too much? Would it be too commercialized? There is little talk among the pilgrims now save for how close we are to our goal.

I felt my whole body being pulled toward Santiago, every sign for Santiago like a blessing and even catching a glimpse of the hills above it now was thrilling. It almost felt as if it were the home we had never seen.

Confessions: We had completely given up the pretense of taking each day as it came or walking in a relaxed manner.

Day 33. Arzúa to Arca do Pino: 19.2 km (12 miles)

After our long walk yesterday, this seemed like a stroll. We couldn't find our pensión so we ended up at what I hoped was my last albergue. I had developed a paradoxical relationship with these. On one hand, I loved the communal nature and the improbable ways we got to know each other and share the joys and trials of this pilgrimage. Staying in the albergue was like staying at a private club in that you had to have a pilgrim passport to enter. There the likeness ended. I was weary of bunkbeds, night sounds, smelly clothes, overused bathrooms, and noise. I was tired even of trying to make conversation in different languages. I wondered if it was because we were at the end of the trip, and I was preparing myself to let go of the Camino.

I've noticed that when people are planning to move from Alaska, they suddenly see everything about it that is difficult. They begin to remember the distance you have to fly to get anywhere, the dark cold winters, the icy streets, and all the other grudges. They forget the beauty and adventure as if they must, in order to be able to let it go and see the good of where they are going.

So it seemed I was acting as we neared the end of the Camino.

That night a group of Germans cooked up a gourmet meal of seafood and vegetables. It looked wonderful.

Confessions: Steve and I went to a little restaurant and ordered what was the telltale sign that we were yearning for a change—a hamburger.

Day 34. Arca do Pino to Santiago: 20.6 km (12.9 miles)

Perhaps I slept that night for an hour or two. But the stereophonic snoring and the rustling of the twenty or so teenagers made for a short night. When the youth leaders starting waking their group at four o'clock, I figured if you can't beat 'em, join 'em. So Steve and I got up too, packing as quietly as we could, shining our flashlights to look for anything under the bed, and tying up our laces one more time. The laces on my boots had worn down to the string, my nylon pants sagged with the constant wear, and my baseball cap was brown with dirt. I shouldered my backpack that morning, wanting to carry it on the final leg of the pilgrimage, although Steve had taken most of the weight in his.

The pack of teens, evidently a church group trying to make it to Mass in Santiago, had left ahead of us in the blackness of the night. As luck would have it, we'd lost one headlamp and depleted the batteries on the other. So on that last morning of our five-hundred-mile walk we couldn't see five feet in front of us!

Then I remembered I'd thrown in a tiny LED light that I usually had clipped to my car keys. I dug it out, and by its small beam, we began our last day, looking again for those yellow arrows that had become our silent steady fingers pointing us toward home.

When we entered the woods, we could hear the teens ahead of us but couldn't tell which way to go. We swung the little light around until we found the yellow arrow low on a stone. Although we always appreciated these markers and felt their small but constant assurances to us on this trip, that morning they became more precious to us when we had to search carefully to find them. Arrow by arrow they had led us over the Pyrenees and across Spain. Now on our final day, the darkness of the morning reminded us of how little we had known about our way beforehand. We had to rely on knowing only yellow arrow to yellow arrow, a different spiritual practice of being present in the moment. And we remembered when I had lost my way during the storm by not paying attention, distracted by fear and physical discomfort. On this very last day of being a pilgrim (in the formal sense), I could acknowledge that fear and discomfort are not so much to be resisted as acquiesced to for their part in transformation.

As we shuffled along in those dark stands of eucalyptus trees, I was glad to start our last day in this way, walking in darkness, knowing the light would come.

And so did the rain. Once again we donned our raingear and leaned into the wind that hit us as we came out of the woods and crossed under the airport runway that lies outside of the city. As dawn seduced the darkness, the outline of the city appeared, and my spirits soared despite my soggy feet. When I remembered the many times the rain and wind had challenged us on this journey, I realized that they had also made this trip a true pilgrimage. It was those tests by nature that now defined and embroidered some of the most significant parts of our journey and certainly heightened our joy for the simplest of things—warmth, food, shelter.

It was so early on a Sunday morning that no shops were open, so we walked 14.4 kilometers before finding a little store where we could have morning coffee, tea, and dry biscuits. When we left the café, the sun had come out and an entourage of equestrians galloped by us heading for the city. We began to meet and greet pilgrims we had known along the way, taking pictures of each other, sharing our feelings of regret

Marcia at Santiago marker

and joy as the Camino was nearing the end. Then we crested the hill and saw the last bridge before the outskirts of town and the sign that said, "Santiago."

I nearly felt like skipping now. It surprised me how my happiness welled up from a deep place in my soul as we walked toward the spires of the cathedral. I knew that thousands and thousands of pilgrims had walked that street, but that day, I was sure no one felt it as I did.

We crossed the last busy intersection and headed down the narrow street, hearing then the sound of distant bagpipes. Their eerie wailing matched my soul as we grew closer and closer, keening to end this journey, whatever it had been, however it had been. As the notes pierced us, we passed under the arch before the plaza of Obradoiro and into the throng of people. Only a few more steps remained across the flat stones. No more mud or manure, no more stumbling rocks or uphill slopes. No more.

We walked into that plaza that spread out widely and generously in front of our destination—the Santiago de Compostela Cathedral, the Cathedral of St. James, where (perhaps) the body entombed was the body of the disciple James who walked with Jesus.

I didn't know whether to run to the center or slow down for those last final steps. My heart was so full of gratitude and regret. As we reached the center of the plaza and then turned to see the face of the cathedral, the low clouds parted and rays of sunshine fell down on us. No matter what, it was blessed. Tears welled up in my eyes, and I felt a new kind of joy that tumbled inside of me and felt like it was lifting me up off the ground. We had arrived. We hugged. We kissed. We had someone take our picture.

And then we were simply stunned. It was over. No more days to check off in our guidebook. No more days of being a pilgrim on the Camino. No more necessary kilometers to walk. We had walked from St. Jean Pied Pont to Santiago, five hundred miles, just as we hoped, dreamed, planned, and prepared.

Now what?

*Santiago Cathedral—the end of our journey or
the beginning of a new one?*

Feeling a little lost with no yellow arrow or scallop shell to guide us, we walked over and just sat on the stone benches on the side of the plaza and looked at the ornate cathedral. The statue of St. James on horseback high on the façade, the delicate spinnerets, the carved arches, the old gray, weathered stone. It was about ten o'clock in the morning, and the pilgrim Mass would be at noon. I knew then that we would go to the church service, of course. Now it seemed obvious. But first we needed to check in at the pilgrim office, present our much-stamped and frayed pilgrim passports, and get our certificates of completion. Then to find the place we would call home for a few days.

The guidebook suggested a pensión called Estrella that was close to the plaza. I liked the name, meaning "star." After a couple of wrong turns, we found it tucked in a corner, down a small flight of steps just off the plaza. They had a room that would open in a few hours, and we were allowed to leave our backpacks in the hall. We slipped out of our boots and into sandals and set out to make the final steps of our trip into the cathedral itself.

It had been the ancient custom to place your hand on the tall, carved column at the entrance of the cathedral upon arrival; the years of custom had worn a deep handprint into the stone. But now, it was cordoned off from the pilgrims, so we could only look. Then we entered the sanctuary and realized that there must have been a High Mass at ten o'clock that was just ending. The cathedral was packed with worshippers, and as I stepped into the crowd, I was pushed along until suddenly it seemed the crowd parted, and I was looking at the ecclesiastical recessional coming right at me—the acolytes, the crucifer holding up the tall golden cross, the bearer of the huge red Bible with gold lettering, the priest with his headdress, the many other assisting priests in their chasubles, the altar boys. There it was—all that I loved and distrusted—the hierarchy and tradition of the church coming right at me. I literally was pushed by the crowd into the bishop leading the procession. He stopped, looked at me, and scowled. I wanted to laugh. It couldn't have been a mere coincidence that I faced the thing I had complained about for so long—the patriarchy of the church.

I saw God's sense of humor immediately. I had wrestled with my decision to resign as parish pastor a few months prior to the Camino, feeling both relief and regret at the decision, both grateful and discouraged by my experience in equal measure. On that final day, when the sun shone and the bagpipes played, when I confronted that which I had resented the most on this trip, I was brought to see it face to face. And I had a strange sense of calm. I wanted to tell him, "You need me. The feminine." But he couldn't hear or understand me. Yet I felt no need to defend against all that the bishop represented. I had this thought: "It is what it is." I could not label it good or bad, beautiful or ugly. It simply was. And I was in the midst of it. In an instant it seemed my resentment melted and forgiveness happened, both toward myself and toward the church. I didn't see a vision of St. James there in the sanctuary of the Santiago cathedral, but any time forgiveness comes—and comes that quickly—it must be miracle.

A little dazed by this revelation and still amused, I found one of the few wooden pews available for the next Mass where Steve and I, bone tired, could sink down on the thin, wooden slats. It had only been a 12-mile walk, but the sleepless night was catching up with us, or perhaps the force of emotion or simply the compilation of thirty-four days of pilgrimage.

I sank into the back of the seat, Steve close beside me as more people slid in, squeezing together. I looked up at the soaring arches and the golden pipes of the organ. The sanctuary teemed with people as more and more pilgrims and tourists crowded in. Some were kneeling at confession in dark booths on the side, some taking pictures, some standing in line to view the tomb of the man that caused all this commotion in the first place—St. James. But we sat, grateful for a seat and still a little numb to the fact that we were really here.

The packed Pentecost pilgrim Mass inside the cathedral

I noticed then that a woman speaking German shuffled into the crowd to sit right at the end of our pew. She had a little foldout chair to sit on. *Of course*, I thought, *those Germans are always prepared.* What slightly disconcerted me was that the woman sat so she was facing me more than the front of the church. I felt as if I was being stared at, so I smiled and then averted my eyes as quickly as I could. Perhaps she was looking at someone over my head. But when I looked again, she was looking at me, steadily and patiently as if waiting for me to recognize her.

About twenty minutes before the Mass began, a cantor came out and in several languages explained that we would be having a little song practice so that we could all join in the service when the time came. The songs were in Latin, another universal language. I was particularly delighted when the cantor introduced the Taize chant called "Ubi Caritas" as the communion hymn. It was the same words and tune that I had been singing all along the Camino during the past weeks. The words translated mean, "Where true charity and love abide, God is dwelling there, God is dwelling there." I don't really remember much of the service. Most of the pilgrims were waiting for the big *fumero* to swing over the crowds. Really, a big incense burner, the fumero was designed to swing on thick ropes anchored overhead, not so much as an aid to worship as an aid in dispelling the body odor of the pilgrims. But the fumero was being repaired, one rope deemed too unsafe.

When we got to communion time, I closed my eyes and sang the Taize chant, letting the familiar words assure and comfort me. I loved singing in this huge place with hundreds of others joining me in the chant. It was as if we were already in communion even before we had received the bread and wine. When I opened my eyes as the chant ended, the German woman was looking at me, her face shining and smiling. As we stood to share the peace, she grabbed me and gave me a big hug, saying, "You sing like the angels."

Another bowling ball of enlightenment came rolling down the alley toward me. Almost the entire way I had held a stubborn grudge against the Germans on the Camino. I had been irritated by their efficiency, their seemingly too perfect clothes and walking gear, their maddening habit of being up first and walking the fastest. Their competitiveness to take the beds at the albergues and the chairs at the pilgrim restaurants. But as the words of the chant still rang in my head, I realized two things. I was German; my father's side is German as far back as the generations could be traced. Half of my genes came from German stock, but I only claimed the Norwegian side, perhaps because of my mother's influence. But there I came to realize that the Germans irritated me because I was getting a mirror to my own shadow and my own prejudices and need for perfection. And even more significantly, I had been rejecting a part of my own self, a part that evidently was insistent on being claimed.

I also realized that I had carried my need to separate myself from "those Germans" all the way into the cathedral, avoiding connection with the German woman who had sat down near me. Yet I had sung of charity and love and the dwelling of God in the midst of us. And it was a German woman who had blessed me and hugged me. She had understood the words when I had not. I would believe it if someone told me she was an angel come to teach me this important lesson at the end of the Camino. Why did she look only at me?

I had to come face to face with my persisting competitiveness on the Camino, a far cry from true charity and love. I remembered that I never felt whole when trying to overtake someone or be first to the albergue. I had felt myself when I was serving or laughing or stopping to take a picture of a scene that filled me with awe. I had been competitive physically, particularly the day I had walked so very fast trying to show up those two old rude Frenchmen who wouldn't let a woman pass.

And I had been a spiritual snob, in some kind of spiritual competition, believing that somehow Steve and I were doing it more correctly than others. Oh God, it was such a humbling trip! Vowing over and over to walk in a relaxed manner only to succumb to my fear and worry and hurry.

The priest ended the service by calling out the numbers of pilgrims from each country who had registered that day at the pilgrim office. I heard Estados Unidos de America and knew we were one of those included in the number. All these countries and languages—again. I couldn't help but be struck by the beautiful synchronicity of arriving here on Pentecost. Perhaps in some way walking the Camino would bind people together as it did at the first Pentecost as told in Acts 2 of the Bible. Perhaps there could be a new understanding even as war raged in Iraq and Afghanistan. As I got up to leave the sanctuary, I felt my muscles, stiffened and tired, my feet, sore and swollen, and my ego, severely bruised by the realizations of my blindness.

I walked out, with regrets, thinking of all the ways I would do it differently next time. Then I nearly stumbled upon a Muslim woman begging at the door of the cathedral, her burqa dirty and worn, holding out her brown hand for a few coins. I was propelled past her in the momentum of the crowd, but for a brief moment I looked into her eyes and she in mine.

"We are all beggars." These were the words found on a scrap of paper in the pocket of Martin Luther, the founder of my faith tradition, just after he died. I didn't remember them at the moment I looked into the eyes of that woman; I was too numb that day. But now I see her and the German woman who hugged me, the Japanese woman who fell and hurt her knee by the fountain, the South African woman who drank Scotch and tried to stand on her head, Juana who took us in during the storm, the British woman grieving her husband, the priest at San Juan de Ortega who nurtured us with soup and words, the passionately intense pilgrim returning from Santiago with a staff in hand—each person I met now flashed into my consciousness, each face and expression, each act of kindness and indifference, each conversation both passionate and cynical—each memory of the trees, and frogs, and richly tilled earth all reminded me that, in the end, as we walk out the door, we are one. We are all begging, each person, each part of creation, to become one again with the Source of all creation. We tread our ways upon this earth, each in our unique Camino, back to that Source, yearning, yearning to become real again. Our souls begging to shed our skins of fear and pride, to lift the lid that has taken captive our light, to open our hearts to love where love is undeserved, and to create sanctuaries on this earth where all are welcomed, just as we beg to belong.

Why did I walk the Camino? To become a beggar again, free of illusions about life and of myself, accepting of what is offered to me in this all too brief but amazing time as a human being, and humble enough to sit and wait at the door, knowing I am not separate from anyone else, whether German or Brazilian or Iraqi, Christian or Muslim or pagan, man or woman or bending tree. I wanted to sink deeper into the holy communion of life on earth, that can be heaven now, and have my eyes open to see it. And I wanted to learn to love again, with a heart that holds all things sacred, with a heart that beats steadily, relentlessly with courage.

There is more. There is always the more. But this beggar woman has begun to see that each day I get up from my bunk and walk the kilometers needed to take me to the next town. Each day there are yellow arrows that will guide me if I pay attention. Each day I will get tired, perhaps have pain, but I can keep walking toward Santiago. Each day I will be given the divine choice to look away or to love. Each day I can cling to my need to be right, or I can forgive myself and others.

I looked at the faces of so many paintings, sculptures, carvings, and symbols of the Holy on this journey. From crosses made of twigs in a chain-link fence to soaring arches gilded in gold. I saw the tomb of St. James, too, the supposed goal of the Camino, and I saw the faces of the penitent at confession. Perhaps it was the wash of all these images that changed me, for I am changed. A woman who is a member of my meditation group told me, six months after that day I saw the beggar woman at the Santiago cathedral, that I am different. "It's as if you found that soft spot inside you again."

May it be so. May that be the final benediction of that long, amazing pilgrimage that found me in a dream—the Camino de Santiago.

Welcome to the Listening Post

Welcome to a quiet space,
made sacred by your
presence.

Listen to your inner wisdom,
as you sit in silence,
meditate or pray.

If you wish to talk one-on-one,
someone is available who will
listen with compassion,
respect, and in
confidence.

May we all come true.

MEGAN MCKENNA

I Will Hold the People
in My Heart

When we returned from the Camino, Steve and I had such a different sense of distance and time that when we were arranging a pickup from the airport, we realized from Google maps that it was 15 miles from our house.

"Oh," said Steve, "we can just walk home!" And it seemed reasonable to both of us. We weren't quite ready to return to the familiar way of being in the world. Already we were talking of going back to the French part of the Camino so we would end up in St. Jean Pied Pont instead of starting there.

Friends with the key to our house had slipped in and put up a big welcome home banner pronouncing, "YOU DID IT! Congratulations!" There were gifts of flowers and food in the fridge. It was so good to return just as Alaska was greening up, and the days were already sixteen hours long. I had kept a blog frequently on the trip so most of my friends and family had followed along with us, and I didn't have to tell the whole story of our journey, even if I could have. I was still in the transition of not having yellow arrows and scallop shells to show me the way. Yet the Camino had done its work. I had come closer to my real self. I had faced many barriers. I had leaned in closer to God and discovered God everywhere. Can my seeking to know the Divine be a mosaic—beautiful pieces or glimpses of God I cannot know and cannot control? Can it be that which I seek is also within me—is *me?*

I was coming closer in my quest, to satisfying that long yearning. What freedom it would be to let God be God and to simply enjoy a glimpse of the Holy as intimately as holding a child, as the enthusiasm of a red-haired woman, as a yellow scallop shell on a moss-covered stone, as pouring rain and raging wind, as losing my way, as waving wheat fields, as a stork on its high steeple nest, as passion, as mist, as presence, as old rock, as the ruins of cathedrals, as compassion, as challenge, as a welcome table and food made with love, as cold mountains, as marble sculptures and Renaissance paintings, as candlelight and incense, as Gregorian chant and deep silence. And as death. For in my surrender came all I've been searching for—my humility, my humanity, my desire to love, to have courage, to accept, and to transcend. And to trust, trust, trust the Way will appear.

And so it did.

After coming face to face with patriarchy in the Santiago cathedral, I no longer feared it or felt its power over me. Patriarchy with its inherent hierarchy and emphasis on masculine energy has had its season in the church. But the balance of the feminine will bring completeness to it. I didn't need to defend against patriarchy but to simply stand in my own truth of my calling as a woman ordained in the church. And that is what unfolded when I returned.

A seed had been planted at the Spiritual Director's Conference I attended in British Columbia a month before the Camino. I had listened to a breakout session with a social worker who avocated at what Vancouver called "Ground Zero." She and a nun had begun an outreach called the Listening Post for the homeless in that area. I visited the site later and spoke with her and felt a resonance with this work.

When I returned from the Camino, I put in motion the desire to start this type of outreach in Anchorage, where those marginalized in our city would be respected and heard in a safe environment. It took a year to finally get all the paperwork, insurance, blessing by the church governing body, and a formal call from the bishop to open the door of the Listening Post of Anchorage in 2008. I had learned how to work with the patriarchy. The vision became a thriving and welcoming place in the city center with twenty-five eager volunteers and over twenty-five hundred visits from the marginalized community that first year. It wasn't that I hadn't done some work to get it started and keep it going, but I learned from experience that the Listening Post had its own energy, wisdom, and purpose. I just followed it along—once again, the Wayless Way.

As it unfolded it was shaped by the volunteers and their deep love of the visitors and the visitors themselves. Everyone was welcome. The community was diverse. The premise was compassion. And there was no hierarchy. No liturgical worship marked this place, but there were daily rituals: visitors wrote about their lives in the journal, some recited their own poetry, some played the singing bowl or walked the labyrinth

The welcoming sign outside the Listening Post of Anchorage in the Transit Center

The cozy interior of the Listening Post, where all were welcomed

on the floor. Many sat quietly, some talked back to the voices in their heads, some meditated. Some prayed. Some were angry. Many were sad. Some told jokes. Some drank tea. And many shared their stories. Both volunteers and visitors began saying the Listening Post was their church. When it first happened, I was surprised. I even questioned that naming. But then I shifted and saw it was indeed the church I had been called to serve. It should have been obvious, but it wasn't. In a path I could not have anticipated or planned, I was staying true to the vow I took at my ordination—to "hold the people in my heart." I was restless no more.

What a long journey it had been, to feel that church was my home and belonging place, yet to lose that connection in college and the decade after. Then to find church as home again, eventually as a pastor, only to resign and walk a pilgrimage with the same search. How ironic to have found home at the Listening Post with a community that was "home-less." More deeply, to find that home did not really depend on anything external; it was available within.

It was all homecoming. It had been from the beginning. And would be as the path beckoned me on. For now I knew, the longing always calls me on to a deeper walk, a greater trust, and a more wondrous knowing of Love.

With Gratitude

Writing this book was a pilgrimage in itself, and I want to thank those that walked with me on this subsequent journey.

To my long-time writers' group of KAYLENE JOHNSON-SULLIVAN, ANN DIXON, and LAURA COOK who were the midwives for the book, laboring with me during revision after revision and always encouraging its birth.

To my editors, ANDROMEDA ROMANO-LAX and JOETH ZUCCO who steadied the writing and helped it grow up.

To MELISSA ALGER for her exacting proofreading and final polishing of the book.

To my readers JEANINE HEATH-GLINN, JAN GRIFFIN, AVENUE WATERS, and SHERRY ANDERSON who kept me going.

To NANETTE STEVENSON for her wise and tender care in designing the manuscript into a book and seeing the shape of its soul.

To KAYLENE JOHNSON-SULLIVAN and EMBER PRESS for its generosity of spirit in bringing this book to print.

To STEVE, who not only carried my pack on the Camino, but has said yes to all my spiritual wanderings.

To my children, JACK and KARRIE, and my grandchildren REAGAN, MASON, and HATTIE who have always inspired my writing.

And, to my high school English teacher, MURIEL VETTER, who was the first to look me in the eye and say, "You will write."

MARCIA WAKELAND enjoys her life as a writer, an advocate of listening and a longtime Alaskan. She lives in Eagle River Valley with her family and still loves to walk. She has written two children's books: *The Big Fish: An Alaska Fairy Tale* and *Loon Song*. She also served as a writing consultant for the Anchorage School District.

CPSIA information can be obtained
at www.ICGtesting.com
Printed in the USA
JSHW052308050622
26714JS00004B/12

9 780998 688374